TEACHERS AND
MENTAL HEALTH

TEACHERS AND MENTAL HEALTH

The art of accurate speech and other ways to help students (children) not become psychiatric patients.

James E. Campbell, M.D.

authorHOUSE®

AuthorHouse™
1663 Liberty Drive
Bloomington, IN 47403
www.authorhouse.com
Phone: 1-800-839-8640

First published by AuthorHouse   06/20/2011

ISBN: 978-1-4634-1025-4 (sc)
ISBN: 978-1-4634-1024-7 (dj)
ISBN: 978-1-4634-1426-9 (ebk)

Library of Congress Control Number: 2011908581

Printed in the United States of America

Teachers and Mental Health:
The art of accurate speech and other ways to help students (children) not become psychiatric patients.

Book 3 in the Rapid Relief Series

Mental health recommendations for teachers and parents

Hint:

Teaching children to speak accurately can eliminate a huge number of adult mental problems

I dedicate this book to Mrs. Kimbrough and Royce Devick, (two of the many Warsaw High School teachers that pushed me to succeed); Doctors Knight and McCarthy (without who's help I am not certain I would have made it through medical school) along with Dr. Edward Auer and Dr. Felix (who I considered friends as well as mentors); Dr. Tarlow, (Northwestern University Chicago who gave me my first look at what a psychiatrist might do), Doctors Ted Reid, Ed Wolpert, Roy Grinker, and Dan Offer (Who shaped my initial understanding of psychiatry at Michael Reese); Dr. Dennis Cantwell and Fred Gottlieb (UCLA Child Fellowship), and all of the other teachers in my life (mainly the patients who have stuck with me until I got things right) that have contributed along the way to my being able to succeed.

I also dedicate this book to my father Ernest Campbell, and my mother Mildred Campbell, who both taught me essential lessons about life over their entire lives.

ABOUT THE AUTHOR

James Campbell, M.D. was born in Beardstown, Illinois. He graduated co-valedictorian from Warsaw High School; then he attended MacMurray College in Jacksonville, Ill. for three years before being accepted to St. Louis Univ. Medical School, He then went to Michael Reese in Chicago for a one year medical internship and his basic three year adult psychiatric residency. In 1971, after two years in the Air Force, he set up a private practice in Phoenix, Arizona. It was in the Air Force that he had an opportunity to teach several classes in psychology to military dependents also stationed at Ramey AFB, Puerto Rico. As a part of his psychiatric practice Dr. Campbell had many opportunities to participate in hospital staff education programs, and along with Gary Emery Ph.D., Larry Waldman Ph.D., and Kent Leigh Ph.D. he participated in numerous conferences in Phoenix. He was always interested in techniques that might speed up the process of therapy.

In 1980 he completed a 2 year child fellowship at UCLA and added the treatment of children to his practice. He also discovered that he could teach many of the ideas in this book to his patients with a good result. Because of that success, he took a chance and started teaching patients more concepts. This resulted in quicker improvements. Many of these concepts evolved over the years, and they just make good sense in taking care of day to day issues. Because a lot of children and adults did not seem to be in possession of the concepts, it had to be assumed that the educational system was not addressing these concepts. The positive reception by most of his patients and their families encouraged him to undertake the writing of this book intended for teachers, parents, educators and Oprah Winfrey.

OVERVIEW:
THE DILEMMA OF BEING
DELUSIONAL

Teachers (parents), are you aware younger children (less than 12 years of age) are delusional? You may have had reason to think something was wrong with the majority of children, but you may not have figured out what it was.

In psychiatry, we have a form of thinking referred to as a <u>delusion</u>. It is essentially a false belief that is not altered by reasonable arguments. It is a symptom of certain forms of mental illness. I speculate a minimum of half of the world is in a delusional state of being all the time, and most likely 98% of the people in the world respond to a situation in a delusional fashion at least one, or more, times during an average day. All of these people obviously do not have a mental illness. This is a developmental issue.

This will be a topic for a larger discourse later, so I will only give a sample here. Children believe others are responsible for their thoughts, their feelings and their actions. This is not an accurate perception. It is a delusion. When children grow up, they take this belief system with them into adulthood. Many children are taught by the people close to them to act as if this way of thinking is accurate, and those members of society frequently end up in prison when their behavior can no longer be ignored. If they escape prison, they are still doomed to a life of conflict and turmoil.

I used to question why so many prison inmates claimed they had done nothing wrong. It is actually fairly simple; they are delusional. They still think the same way they did as a child; if you look at their behaviors from within the cognitive system they use, their actions may seem appropriate. If I believe you have the power to make me mad, and if I believe you have made me angry, it is logical for me to do something to you to impress you to stop your (perceived) assault against me. We do not label this form of delusion a mental illness, although we do often call the resulting behaviors a mental condition: oppositional defiant disorder, conduct disorder, antisocial disorder, episodic dyscontrol syndrome, some depressions and some anxiety—the list goes on. Even though we have all experienced it, it is still not accurate; because we all do it, it is not called a delusion. If we called it a delusion, we might try to do something about it. Instead we ignore it until it reaches an extreme point, and then we punish the person who mistakenly acts out on their erroneous beliefs (doing what they feel they should).

Teaching a few specific concepts to children <u>could</u> correct this problem.

I have, at times, included a potentially heated point of view for the reader to consider. I was going to go through and eliminate these to make the book less challenging, but then I thought, *"I am attempting to get people to think more critically, and at the same time more thoroughly and rational. Why should I take out those common, but irrational, situations we must deal with daily?"* Instead, I have chosen to leave them in, and I hope you will recognize them, and you will understand it is perfectly ok with me if you reason through them differently than I do; but see if you can stay out of the immediate emotional reaction a comment may seem to provoke.

If you do not make an effort to use the information, my objective in writing this type of a book will have been lost. I know you are not going to be able to go to the Board of Education and get approval to include what I am promoting into any lesson plan. What I am promoting has to do with the way you teach what you teach. It has to do with listening to your children and helping them to understand not only the lessons from their texts, but also the lessons about life you can impart to them. To do so, **you must know the principles yourself.**

In the manner of a teacher, I will address some concepts several times in this book, because I feel they are important.

Schoolroom teachers are underpaid and over worked, but they should be aware they have an opportunity to benefit the world far more than they do currently. This can be done by teaching themselves and their pupils how to make accurate sentences, and by helping students to understand what sentences do not make sense. Adding these elements creates for the student a more realistic world: a world with fewer burdens and more joys. Parents must also understand these concepts, or they will erase any benefit the teacher creates, when the child comes home.

I will be using teacher and parent interchangeably throughout the rest of this book. Both are teachers of children.

Young children are, as a whole, willing to learn, but they are less willing to learn concepts like responsibility and accountability from the parents. Children do not always see their parents as teachers. Children and parents too often get caught up in an *"I am right; you are wrong"* configuration. This does not result in a good product. The timing of this conflict can be at any age, but seems to be focused between 10.5 years and 15 years of age for most children.

I am certain if you are a teacher, or parent, and are reading this you will want to say, *"But I have been trying to teach my pupils (children) responsibility and accountability and is it not working."* There are several reasons it may not be working. One is because the definition of responsibility, as it appears in the dictionary, is so confusing; it really does not work. (The confusion is an example of what is known as fallacy of equivocation. Equivocation is when a word has two meanings, which can be, and frequently are, misunderstood when the word is used.) One might believe teaching responsibility and accountability, and other related topics, should be the parent's job. It is hard to argue against this view, but it has some problems; parents may not be good developmental scientists; they frequently do not have an understanding of when children can learn concepts. Teachers hopefully have a better

3

working knowledge of childhood development, and they can be helpful to parents in this area.

Most adults are not good at reasoning. In our society, we have a lot of stereo-types for people who do not reason well: *she is just blonde, his brain is between his legs.* It is sad, but most people do not think very accurately. It is not easy to do when we deny the obvious, when we see only what we want to see, when we let our feelings, or our biases, overrun our judgment, and when we do not make an effort to think through the consequences of either our thoughts or our actions. We project our own biases and beliefs into situations, often without truly considering the reality, or the options. People hear selectively, and they seldom absorb everything they need to make good judgments. Arguments are too infrequently solved by reason. In conversations most people cannot separate relevant from irrelevant data. Why?

You may, or may not, be familiar with the reference to levels of abstraction, or as some writers refer to it, ladder of abstraction, so let me elaborate briefly. Levels of abstraction run from the very low level, observable phenomena, like the salivation of a dog to the ringing of a bell (Pavlov) to the high level intellectual concept of the *"one true form."* (Plato)

In the real world, you might look around and see how many places you can identify as a place to sit. If you asked the next five people who come into the room to do the same thing you would likely have a pretty good level of agreement (this is a low level abstraction question).

Now look around the room and see if you can identify places to sit which you think are better than others. This moves us up the ladder. We might find when we ask our friends what places they think are better, there is a different level of agreement (good and better are higher levels of abstraction).

Next look around and choose the one best place to sit. See if others agree with you. It is expected you would have even less concurrence with the answers now, because people will define best according to their own personalities: those liking to watch TV might choose the seats facing the TV, readers might choose the chair with the best lighting, mildly paranoid people might like the chair facing the door, and so it goes (this is abstraction at a higher level).

In the act of educating children or adults, much of what we are presenting as information to students can be understood as moving back and forth along the axis of abstraction. Much of science involves taking a high level abstract idea, and then devising a test to prove the idea at the experiential level. When we can observe something directly, it moves the idea from the high level abstraction to a lower level of abstraction. Light has mass. [High level abstraction] Gravity has been shown to affect mass. [Once a high level abstraction concept, now an observable phenomenon] Show how light is bent by gravity, and you prove light has a mass. This was done by observing the behavior of light as it moves around the moon when the moon gets between the earth and the sun. Light behaves as if it has mass.

Response-ability vs. responsibility

Imagine my placing a pen on the desk in front of us and asking you the question, *"Who is responsible for the pen staying on the desk?"* Think what your answer might be before reading further.

I get as many as 15 different answers from people: *nobody, whoever put it there, you, gravity, whoever cleans up for you, whoever bought the pen, whoever brought the pen into the office, the pen itself, etc.* These answers are all high level abstraction answers and none of them really address response-ability.

For the remainder of this book when I write responsibility I will be referring to the word as it is currently defined in a dictionary.

The form I will use when referring to the way I suggest responsibility should be understood will be response-ability.

The word responsibility unfortunately has two meanings intrinsic to it: response-ability and assigned accountability. The answers people commonly give to my question are assignments of accountability. These responses are high level abstractions, which is why there are so many differing ones. If I were to rephrase the question to *"Who in this room can take the pen off of the desk?"* everyone would respond, *"We all can."* This is a very low level abstraction question; it has a very high level of agreement. Responsibility has both a high and a low level abstraction meaning, and people in general do not know which one is in play when the word is being used. Whenever a word has two or more different meanings, the resulting confusion is called ambiguous or a fallacy of equivocation.

A restructuring of the definition of responsibility can help people solve individual problems: **if you say it correctly, you believe it correctly; if you believe it correctly, you will act on it appropriately.**

The comment is made: *"You make me mad!"* If we look at it with the current meaning of responsibility, it suggests the person being referred to as you has caused the feeling of anger in the other person. This is actually an assignment of accountability, and it has nothing to do with causality. It is inaccurate speech, and it suggests a relationship between you and my being mad which is not accurate. When people make the mistake of believing there really is a relationship, it sets the stage for failure, frustration, loss of self-esteem, self-criticism, and of course litigation. It also prevents the correct person from working on the problem; the problem is not solved; the problem is only made worse. *"You hurt my feelings,"* is a prototype sentence, and it includes almost everything characteristic of inaccurate speech. It implies cause and effect where there is none. It reflects the belief that others are responsible for my feelings. Both interpretations make this inaccurate. Not only is the sentence inaccurate, but the idea behind the sentence will go on to cause a lot more problems in life than the grammatically incorrect sentence, *"You makes me mad."*

"The devil made me do it." In this case the devil could be replaced with my brother, my sister, my mother, my father, my teacher, etc. It is inaccurate speech. Sometimes children will tell their teachers they do not know why they act the way they do (poking someone with a pencil), or they will give some answer they think will be accepted by the teacher. *("He left it on my desk, so I just kept it.")*. These are legitimate

answers from younger children who are trying to put some reason on their actions. It is legitimate because children really do not understand mental intermediation. Many adults do not understand it either. It is contra-productive to get angry with a child for these answers. It is an opportunity to help them understand their mental processes. As Barksdale (<u>Building Self-Esteem</u>) asserts, we always do what the sum of our thoughts tell us is the best action at the time. We can never do better than the best assessment we can make.

Children who maintain the devil made them do it, need to learn to state their answer more accurately: *"I do not know why I did it."* This may have been the first answer they gave, but when it was not accepted they went on to try and manufacture an answer satisfactory to the adult asking the question. When we move away from seeing emotions as intelligent (<u>Emotional Intelligence</u>-Daniel Goleman) we can almost always identify the thought, or type of thinking, leading to the behavior. Children do not understand mental intermediation, so they do not understand the role their own thinking has on their behavior.

Mental intermediation includes the thoughts running around in your mind during the day. As you read, or listen, to a presentation, they are the thoughts in the background: do I like this, do I believe this, do I want to remember this, can I apply this later, etc. These thoughts set up the feeling experiences we have; many times people are not aware of what is running in their head, and they are even less aware of how these thoughts are actually creating their feelings.

The pressures to maintain inaccurate speech are high. As much as I love the sound of country-western music, many of its words are reflective of the worst ways of thinking and communicating. It is full of *"somebody did somebody wrong"* love songs. It has a good rhythm, but a truly unhealthy message. The words are intended to be reflections on the struggles of life, and a lot of the troubles we have are tied to the way we respond, so it makes sense this music would reflect the type of thinking causing the problems in the first place. A careful look will show a major failure to promote response-ability and self accountability. Recent songs do this less. The female song writers seem to be moving more into self accountability wording. There is an entire genre just waiting for someone to run with it.

Speech is an important behavior. I encourage patients to pay close attention to the way they phrase what they say. At times I will suggest certain words not be used at all. The reader already knows I discourage the *"you made me"* phraseology. When we practice staying away from such word construction it will greatly enhance long-term happiness. Before I start a therapy session with someone, I may inform them I will interrupt what they are telling me, if they are using inaccurate language. To allow them to continue to use that form of speech means they continue to create erroneous belief systems while they are talking to me. If I do not interrupt those patterns, it is as if I am in agreement with what they are saying. I do not challenge what they are telling me; I challenge only the inaccurate wording in which the story is being reported. Teachers could do the same thing when they encounter a conflict between children.

Inaccurate speech, as I am using the term, does not have anything to do with the grammatical structure of a sentence, but is about the misleading, inaccurate, or confusing content of a sentence. I am not referring to the easily identified errors a person might make (The first of each month must fall on a Monday), but to the pattern of speech commonly used over and over, but rarely identified as inaccurate speech (*"You are making me mad" "You are driving me crazy"*).

Another component of inaccurate thinking and subsequently inaccurate speech occurs when children and adults do not discern between <u>cause and effect</u> and <u>sequential ordering of events</u>. Children attribute cause to hundreds of thousands of non-causal, sequential events. (The child is playing; mother calls the child in for dinner; the child is unhappy; the unhappiness is attributed by the child to mother calling them in for dinner.) The actual cause of the child's unhappiness is their **mental intermediation**. If the child had been hungry and was looking forward to lunch, they would have been happy with mother summoning them. Either way it is the mental intermediation creating the feeling, not mother calling them to come and eat. This type of error is made over and over. It is a major contributor to inaccurate speech. This is not adequately explained to children. It actually needs to be lived more than explained. Every teacher needs to be ready, by example and through personal vigilance, to correct this error.

Can young children learn this concept?

Our three year old granddaughter Katie was talking to her grandmother, but suddenly stopped. Grandmother, being her commonly impatient self, indicated to Katie to finish the sentence. Katie's response was, *"Gramma, my brain has not told my mouth what to say yet."* I am not certain how she made the connection at three, but she was right on. Comments of this type give me hope we can teach children at a young age about mental inter-mediation.

Young children are unable to distinguish cause and effect from sequential ordering of events. Older children, those who can make the distinction, generally do not, because they fail to recognize the importance of doing so, and because most of the people around them are not making the distinction either. A staff member at St. Luke's hospital helped me to understand this better. She brought me a book to look at saying, "I know you are interested in Cause and Effect, and I thought you might like to look at this." The book was titled Cause and Effect. I took it home and looked through it. I was amazed to find there was nothing in the book about cause and effect; it was entirely about sequential ordering of events.

Cause and Effect relationships are generally low level abstraction issues: you step on a nail and there is a painful hole in your foot. One does not have to go to court to figure this one out. Courts are where people go when they want to hold others responsible for something not easily identified as causal, or when someone (attorney or individual) wishes to convince others there is a causal relationship when none exists. More accurately what courts generally do is assign accountability for something to one or more people who are seen as having money. Since we frequently cannot see any connection (It is no longer low level abstraction) between the event and the one being held responsible, it takes a lawyer, who is presumably smarter than the rest of us, to show us the connection. Since the word responsibility has both the high and low level abstraction meaning as currently defined, a jury can sometimes be led to the end product the attorney desires. If we used the concept of responsibility more accurately we could simplify events in court and elsewhere: *"We know there is no response-ability here, but you have money and my client and I want some of it, so we are going to try and get you, the jury, to award us some."*

The inability to differentiate these two concepts leads to people attributing cause and effect to thousands (perhaps millions) of sequential events in nature. The factor present all the time, but not taken into consideration, one of those concepts hidden in the open, is an occurrence of "mental intermediation" between the first event and the second event.

Others are responsible for (cause) my thoughts, feelings and actions; I am responsible for (cause) others thoughts, feelings and actions (system one thinking; S1T) is the common belief system, the operating system, the only game in town, for the child until they are approximately twelve and a half (12.5) years old. This is a blame belief system. It is a bad system of thinking for children, and it creates even greater problems for adults.

This belief is, without a doubt, the most problem-generating concept humans have been harnessed with through the ages.

It is *"the mother of all problem creating ideas."*

This belief system is another major area where teachers/parents have an opportunity to help children make adjustments to their thinking. It could markedly reduce problems for children, and, thereby, in the long run for adults. It would reduce the behavior problems teachers experience. Children younger than twelve do not understand responsibility or cause and effect, so they attribute cause resulting from their mental intermediation to thousands of events which have no causal relationship. Children hold everything, and everybody, responsible for the way they feel, and what they do—except themselves.

Remember this is a delusional system for the first 12 years of a child's life.

It is delusional because it is an inaccurate belief system, and children younger than 12.5 years <u>cannot</u> be talked out of it by reasoning. It stops being a delusion shortly after that age and once children <u>can</u> be talked out of it. If this transition does not occur, the belief system remains an influencing delusional system into adulthood.

[I have often wondered if we actually taught children to speak accurately, if they could get out of this belief system sooner—I do not know the answer.]

Parents complain their five, eight, or ten year old children will not be *"responsible for anything."* They apparently do not have any idea it is not possible for a child of this age to understand concepts like responsibility. This is one of the cases where the expectations may actually contribute to the lowering of self-esteem over time. Teachers can help parents have a more reasonable expectation of their child's capabilities.

Assigning others accountability for something they have no response-ability for is a major way of creating problems. Repeated thousands, perhaps millions of times in childhood, and often even more times in adulthood, because adulthood runs longer than childhood, it creates a social pressure affecting millions of lives, millions of times. It is a form of blaming having little, or no, real substance. The process is often not seen, and the relationship between this form or thinking and multiple negative outcomes is missed by teachers, parents, and even many mental health workers.

Failure to recognize and to help correct this early operating system is the cause of much conflict in childhood, and also later in adulthood.

When it is not corrected in childhood, it becomes a major source of mental health issues in adults.

Easily, eight out of every ten adults coming into my practice for problems related to anger, marital discord, depression, job related problems, issues with their family of origin, and issues with their children are still locked in the early belief system. All my cutters, burners, suicidal and homicidal patients, and those attempting to escape life in general (often through drug use) are locked in this system. It is a repetitive, go nowhere, no light at the end of the tunnel, no learning, energy intensive, problem creating system. I tell my patients, *"I have nothing better to say about this belief system."*

Children do not seem to be able to really understand concepts like response-ability and accountability until they reach the age of formal operations (Jean Piaget), which occurs at about 12 years of life. This is why I believe it is important to start at a very young age teaching children how to speak accurately. If, at an early age, a child is taught to express themselves accurately, it will help eliminate a lot of confusion later in life, when they can have a better cognitive understanding of the concept.

Our 6 year old grandson, Andrew, fell out of his bed during the middle of the night while we were on a camping trip. The next morning, his grandmother told him about how she had picked him up and put him back in bed. His response was, *"No, it did not happen."* His comment was inaccurate and his speech was inaccurate. Typically, this kind of comment would lead to an argument about what was true. This type of experience is actually an opportunity to practice accurate speech. Just as we teach him to say *"thank you"* or *"please,"* he can be taught to express his point of view in a non-argumentative way. If he expresses his experience, *"Grandmother, I do not remember you picking me up,"* his speech is accurate, and it is not argumentative. *"I know you do not remember it, because you never woke up."* We have thousands of opportunities like this in a child's life to help them learn a non-abrasive language which is actually accurate.

Just this week our son-in-law reported a comment made by four year old Katie, *"Daddy, you are either ignoring me, or you are not hearing what I am telling you."* How many adults could express it more elegantly?

I sidestepped slightly the issue of not being able to teach children younger than 11-12 years of age complex concepts like <u>response-ability</u>

and <u>accountability</u>. I do not think we have to teach the <u>concept</u> to get better results. In the same way we teach children to say *"thank you,"* or *"please,"* to help create a more pleasant child, we can teach them other meaningful ways to address situations. I don't think most children who use *"thank you,"* or *"please,"* actually have an understanding as to why they should make polite statements—initially; they do it because they see it is pleasing to the people who are encouraging them to do so. Later in life, when it takes on an internalized meaning, they are already geared up, and ready to maintain the behavior with little additional attention energy. **Habits can be formed before understanding is achieved**.

Response-ability and *accountability* are two separate concepts under the word responsibility. Because both meanings are present, and neither meaning may be specified, it causes ambiguity. Each of these two concepts has attributes. The attributes of response-ability are 1. Choice is the cardinal component. 2. It is constantly in flux. 3. It cannot be shared. 4. It cannot be transferred. 5. It is influenced by internal factors such as IQ, physical strength, attention, and focus. 6. It is influenced by external factors such as equipment, time, and distance. 7. It is a low-level abstraction issue, and, therefore, has a generally high level of agreement.

There are **three attributes of life we are response-able for: <u>our</u> own thoughts, feelings and actions**. There are **three ideas we can sometimes hold ourselves responsible for, or others will gladly hold us accountable for: <u>other's</u> thoughts, feelings, and actions**.

When people accept response-ability for experiences they really do not have any ability to do something about, it sets the person up for failure, guilt and shame, or additionally, as it occurs in the legal field, for judgment and punishment. I have had a large number of couples, families, and even children over the years with conflicts, who, after spending a little time going over responsibility and its two forms, have been able to go home, and by the time I see them again they have worked through their problems.

When the right people work on the correct areas of the problem progress is made.

As long as children, parents, or teachers stay in the blame system of thinking, or confuse who actually has the power to resolve a given situation, progress will be delayed in solving problems.

Once a person understands what they are actually response-able for, they can proceed to a good solution or resolution. We never resolve problems when we are being held accountable, or are being blamed for something we have no ability to do anything about—like someone else's choice to bully, or someone's choice to shoplift. When one tries to resolve problems using dictionary definitions of responsibility, a solution will not occur. The dictionary definition fosters the ambiguity created when the meaning is not clear. Clarifying the meanings attributed to responsibility and accountability often help to restructure relationships and improve interpersonal conflict. We need to change the dictionary definition.

It is rare to hear people use either the word *answerable* or *accountable*. People generally group all their definitions, or understandings, under the word *responsible*.

Children attempt to avoid responsibility for anything. This is because 1) they do not know what the concept means, and 2) they do not believe they have responsibility. Young children (up to about 10 years of age) do not and cannot separate cause and effect from sequential ordering of events. This confusion prevents them from learning their role in the outcome of events. Adults can and should be able to learn the difference. A legalistic approach often confuses the problem, because it works from the assigned accountability side of the equation. It is a furthering of the way children see justice. Children are great assigners of accountability (They think they are assigning response-ability).

For a time in my practice, I would see the parents alone to get basic information; later, I would see the child and obtain information from them. Commonly, a mother and father would bring their 16 year old son to the session because of *"problems getting along with the parents"* and antisocial behavior. When a history was taken from the family, father would say, and mother would agree, their son *"will not be responsible for anything."* A few minutes later, when talking alone with the son, he would say, *"My parents will not let me be responsible for anything."*

Obviously, the parents and their child were using the term differently. Most parents appear to be saying their children will not follow the rules they have laid down, and/or they will not do what the parents want.

What emerged when talking to the adolescent was his feeling his parents were not allowing him to make any <u>choices</u>. He felt when the parents prevented him from making decisions; they left him without any real responsibility. The adolescent does not see following directions as equivalent to being responsible. In fact, the child's idea of responsible is probably more accurate, than is the parents.

How can a different understanding of responsibility and an increase in the awareness of how its current inaccurate use affects families be best understood? The meaning of the word responsibility I suggest families use to work out their problems is response-ability. This means having the capability to act, or not act, having choice, and the presence of awareness. I also suggest being accountable, or answerable, has nothing whatsoever to do with a useful definition of response-ability; they should be, and actually are, totally different concepts.

The manager of a large department store may be answerable to the owner of the store, or accountable, to his Board of Directors for misconduct by an employee under him; although, in reality, he may have lacked the capacity to perceive his employee would do something wrong, nor could he have taken an action before the event to prevent it. Accountability is a construction created by those in authority. It is made up by those with the power to do so. Only coincidentally, does it actually have anything to do with the reality of the situation.

Sometimes parents report how they have given their children responsibility for emptying the trash, and how they have had to keep reminding him to empty it, four or five times, before the trash is finally emptied. What mother and father are transferring to their son is not responsibility, because it existed even before the request was made. What is being transferred is accountability. The parents then proceed to bring it to his attention, over and over, because he is not doing what they want. He is not failing in responsibility; he is failing in accountability. He is not doing the job the way the parents want him to do it, and in the time frame they want him to do it in. If there is a capacity to perceive and to act, there must also be choice, or there is no responsibility. If there is choice the action may be different from what the parent's desire. In the above example, the child is being responsible (he perceives his task and makes a decision not to do it at that time), but the parent, who is holding him accountable, labels him non-responsible because the task is not being done to their specifications. The child realizes he is being given jobs to do under the disguise of building responsibility, but with the exclusion of choice, it only makes him resentful. As parents put more pressure on him to force compliance, the child senses even more he has no control, or choice, in the interaction; he perceives it as devoid of responsibility.

Nothing useful is happening in these exchanges. The situation is no different than it was at the beginning, except it has developed into a larger conflict. All three people still have the response-ability for emptying the wastepaper basket.

Should children be given tasks to do? Of course, but kids are too smart to buy they are being given responsibility in a transaction containing no choice.

A transaction can be structured so growth will occur: there must be recognition, however, that **response-ability is intrinsic** to the situation, and it cannot be changed by assignment. Parents, by virtue of their position at the head of the family, can assign accountability like a corporate president. The parents may couple receiving, or not receiving, an allowance to a given act, or they can make a rule the wastebasket must be emptied before dinner is served. The child now has a choice to make, as well as an action to take. The rewards and costs are defined, and he can practice decision-making. If he chooses to forfeit the allowance, or give up dinner, he has made a choice. There are no false pretenses involved. The lie is gone.

Responsibility is determined by a number of factors. One is the ability to perceive. This ability is related to the intactness of the senses and the ability to integrate knowledge; therefore, response-ability has, at times, some relationship to intelligence. The capacity to act is based on physical characteristics, distance and time, among other attributes. For example, a physically handicapped mother may have less response-ability for the care of her children than a physically capable mother, even if the accountability is the same. A mother who may generally have sole care for her child moves from a position of almost total response-ability, to one of little response-ability, as she leaves the baby in someone else's care to go shopping. On the other hand, her accountability may remain unchanged!

Three people observe a criminal act; one is an 80-year-old arthritic male several feet away. Another is an athletic policeman viewing the crime inadvertently through binoculars from several miles. The third is a crippled woman viewing the act from an apartment window across the street. Each person may have a responsibility to the victim, but their ability to act and the kind of act they can initiate is obviously different.

Let us take this concept into the normal family interaction. Using the definition given, think about where response-ability lies in the following examples

1. A husband arrives home after a hard day's work to find the sink full of dishes and the floors dirty. Who is responsible for washing the dishes and cleaning up the house?
2. Several members of a family notice paper lying on the floor when they return home. Who is responsible for the paper staying on the floor?
3. A child sleeps through his alarm clock and is late for school. Who is responsible?
4. An appointment is missed and the doctor feels rejected and unhappy. Who is responsible for the doctor's unhappiness?
5. The doctor bills the patient for the missed appointment. The patient is unhappy. Who is responsible for the patient being unhappy?

Discussion

1. When the husband becomes aware of the condition, he is response-able for it remaining, or he can change it. He may, or may not, have overlapping response-ability with another person, depending on whether anyone else is aware of the condition and/or is capable of changing it.
2. Everyone who becomes aware of the paper and has the ability to pick it up. (The person who dropped it may not be aware they dropped it.)
3. Unclear—did anyone else hear the clock, was anyone in proximity to do something? To solve the problem he may have to get a louder alarm.
4. The party experiencing the feeling is response-able for their unhappiness as they are the only one who can actually do anything to create a new feeling.
5. The doctor is response-able for the decision to bill the patient for time scheduled and the decision to hold the patient accountable for paying for the time scheduled. The patient is response-able for missing the appointment and how they feel about being billed for the missed appointment.

As can be seen from these examples response-ability becomes a practical term rather than a blame mechanism. The blame mechanism would answer the above questions with different answers. i.e.:

- The wife has responsibility for the house, dishes, etc.: this is actually an assignment of accountability.
- Whoever dropped it: an assignment of accountability.
- The adult has to be responsible: an assignment of accountability.
- The person who missed the appointment: an assignment of accountability.
- The doctor is responsible; he sent the bill: an assignment of accountability.

There are three areas over which all people have response-ability; these are their own thoughts, feelings and actions (TFA). A serious mistake people make is to either hold others responsible for their TFA, or to hold themselves responsible for others TFA. When we do this, we waste a lot of energy, we create a situation in which failure, guilt or shame are the likely outcomes; we confuse who really has the ability to do something about the situation, setting ourselves and others up for guilt, shame and failure.

Response-ability is ability plus awareness.

If a blind man is given the job of turning on the lights at dusk, there may be a problem. He can do the job, but he may not know when dusk occurs. The quadriplegic given the same job has a different problem. He may know when dusk occurs, but will not be able to do the job. With each, their response-ability is limited by either awareness, or ability. All judgments of response-ability need to be measured on these two axes. In our country, which seems bent to punish others, rather than to understand the origin of the problem, this failure of understanding response-ability creates a great deal of misery.

Understanding the real meaning of response-ability has another side. If you are walking down the sidewalk and there is trash on the ground, you have the response-ability to pick it up; you have both the awareness and the ability. If you see a loose dog running into the street, you have the responsibility to find the owner.

In any given situation many people may have the response-ability for doing something.

Theoretically, we can all give to any number of charities. We could all spend time cleaning up the neighborhood. If we tried to take care of all the chores we have response-ability for we would probably never be able to get out of the house, or make it to work. It must become apparent none of us deal with all the items for which we have response-ability. The important awareness here is to recognize we have response-ability in a lot of situations. We should not attempt to shrug it off, or to exploit others because our response-abilities overlap. Each person must decide which of the opportunities they have response-ability for and choose to act on. It works best when we are clear about what we can do something about. It is less clear when one person assigns to another person what they think the other should have response-ability for: *"You are the wife; you should take care of the house."* This is really an assignment of accountability. One person is defining what should be the other's choice of action. This is also why choice is at the core of response-ability. **If we have no choice we have no response-ability**.

It is important to recognize **response-ability is constantly in flux**. If I have a tool in my hand, I have almost 100% of the say about how the tool is to be used. If I lay it down, perceivably, I could lose all ability to determine how it will be used in seconds. If I am at the pool, I can monitor what is happening at the pool. If I fall asleep, or walk inside, I may find I have no idea about what is happening poolside. The speed at which our ability to do something can change is often under-appreciated by people. A child is in a pool; there is a distraction, and then there is a dead child.

Response-ability is the workhorse. It has to do with causality. It is about what one can do without others participation. It is mine. It is yours. No one can give it to me. Either I have it, or I do not have it. I cannot take it from someone else; I cannot give it to anyone else. In other words **response-ability is intrinsic**. It is **inseparable** from the situation as well as being inseparable from the person. It **cannot be transferred**!

Another attribute of response-ability, besides not being transferable, is **it should not be assigned** unless cause and effect can be proven and choice is/was present. Of course this is what attorneys, children and those with anger problems do all the time. We are not able to assign response-ability for the same reasons we cannot transfer response-ability. It is intrinsic. Because it is intrinsic, it is reasonable for people to own what they think, feel, and do.

What seems most consistent about the physical universe is it is in constant change: in a similar manner **response-ability is constantly in transition**. What I can do at one moment may not be possible a moment later. What I could not do yesterday, I may be able to do today. Just getting up and moving from one place to another alters the entire range of what <u>was</u> possible, and it opens up a whole new book of what <u>is</u> possible.

Response-ability is awareness plus capability. This means **if our awareness increases so does our response-ability**. **If our capability increases so does our response-ability**. These are a part of our intrinsic make up. Capability may mean an intellectual aspect, or a physical aspect: awareness may mean knowledge, or experience.

There are times when **tools** may determine, or greatly influence, the outcome of a given situation. The man with the 45 caliber pistol in his hand may have more to say about what goes on in a room than those without such a device. The man with a backhoe may be able to get the pool dug faster and cleaner than those without equipment. There are times when the entity controlling the finances may determine more of the outcome than can the active participants.

You may have already figured out a lot of people may have overlapping response-ability. Each person brings their unique intrinsic characteristics to any situation, or condition. In any given situation only one person owns their unique perspective of response-ability. Response-ability is about what I can do, not about what I should do

The attributes of assigned accountability are 1. Compliance is the cardinal ingredient. 2. It may be fixed, and frequently is fixed. 3. It can be shared. 4. It can be transferred. 5. Internal, or external, factors do not exert much influence. The exception is possibly the law; at least in some circumstances, the law recognizes diminished capacity. 6. It is a convention; it is made up. 7. It has a higher level of abstraction associated with it (because it is made up) and therefore has a lower level of agreement.

Assigned accountability has to do with the **assignment of causality** to self or others. For example: *"I am responsible for my parent's fights, and their fights are responsible for my feelings."* This meaning of the word responsibility is more accurately understood as assigning accountability to someone, or something. Children like to assign accountability for events to anyone else, regardless of the reality of the situation. You might be sitting at the opposite end of the table when they spill their water, but you will be accused of causing the spill.

Accountability is first of all a **convention**. By this I mean it is **made up**. If your car slips out of gear and rolls back into another car, who will they come looking for? If you said the owner of the car, you would likely be correct. The owner could correctly say, *"I was not there, I should not be held responsible for the accident."* The accurate response would be, *"It is correct, you are not response-able for the accident, but you are being held accountable for the damage."* This could get more interesting if the owner says, *"Actually, I had the car in the garage yesterday for this very problem, and the mechanics told me they had fixed it. I think they should be the ones held accountable for the damage."*

Accountability is different from response-ability in all aspects. Accountability **is often fixed**: sometimes by law (the board of directors may be the accountable body of a corporation), sometimes by religious convention (the woman is to be obedient to her husband), sometimes by tradition (the Pope must be a man), and sometimes for no real perceivable reason at all (*"Why should I pick up this mess?"*).

Accountability **is assignable** as in, *"You watch the kids while I go to the store."* It is not dependent on internal, or external, factors. The guy with the shovel may be as accountable for the pool getting dug, as the person with the backhoe; the student with the average IQ may be expected to get as many right answers on a test to get an A as the genius. There is a consideration called diminished capacity. Theoretically, under the law, children and the mentally disabled are not held at the same level of accountability as normal adults. One should not plan on this consideration in the United States: just a few weeks before this line was written an alert governor did stay the execution of a mentally retarded inmate; the week I wrote this sentence a mentally retarded man was executed. Attorneys are frequently asking to put juveniles on trial as adults, despite their diminished capacity. (A relatively low level abstraction determination if one actually looks beyond the emotional reaction.) If one really took into consideration the cognitive functioning level, many adults ought to be tried as children, because they still conceptualize the world the way children do.

Self accountability, the assignment of accountability to our self, includes two possible areas: one is the area within a circle representing response-ability and the other is the surrounding area where there may be a possibility to influence the event, or the outcome. It is useful to accept accountability in the areas where we have all the power to determine outcome. This is an overlapping with what we are response-able for. It is often even more important to accept some self accountability in the areas of possible influence. This area is not as fixed as is the range of response-ability. It is an area which can be expanded. People can get better at influencing others. If you work on it, you may find other ways to be influential. It is like learning to become the best salesman in a car dealership. In the area of possible influence, however, you are still dependent on other's cooperation. You can become good at presenting the pros and cons of buying the car, but in the end, the person has to be willing to buy, or there is no sale.

Understanding self-accountability helps us learn the relationship between our decisions and the outcomes they create. **Blame is diametrically opposite to self accountability.**

We give up the victim role when we stay accountable for our own feelings. When people accept accountability, they are more inclined to try and understand how they are influencing the outcome. Whether the role is 10% or 90% in any given situation, they look for how they might affect the outcome. People can learn to assume a James Bond attitude toward survival. They can learn to see more clearly the relationship between what they do and what happens in their life. Once we hold our self accountable for what happens to us, we can start getting internal directions on what needs to be done. This is a precursor to building good self-esteem. It should not be confused with self-blame.

It is generally healthy for us to look at how we can better ourselves; how we can become more effective in the area of self accountability. It is possible, however, for the opposite outcome to occur when people are too critical of themselves, or when others are too critical of us. Sometimes parents will not understand the intrinsic limitations of a mentally challenged child, and they will criticize the child into a complete shutdown. Like in most areas of life, if we apply a reasonable yardstick in our measurement, we will get an attitude of reward.

Self accountability influences all areas of our lives. We can greatly influence our health when we hold ourselves accountable for what we eat, whether or not we exercise, and how we relax; whether or not we drink, take drugs, or smoke—all are within our circle of response-ability and will have a direct or indirect influence on our health. The same can be said for nearly all areas of our life.

Properly applying these meanings for responsibility goes a long way to helping people understand, and then to make better choices. There is a rule stating **when I say something I will come to believe what I have said is true; when I believe something I will act on it as if it is true.** This type of mental intermediation needs to be better understood, by children and adults alike.

I heard it said in my child fellowship that girls change best friends seven times more frequently than boys do. What is behind this observation? First of all, girls are more social. Their behaviors are different from boys. For instance they borrow each other's clothes. As a girl, if your friend is not willing to let you borrow what you want, the mental intermediation reflects a belief that she is not really a good friend, she really does not like me, she is stuck up, she probably already loaned it to someone else, or she does not like me best. This easily progresses to the thought, "I certainly will not ever loan her anything again."

This type of event is not as likely to occur with boys who are typically quite happy to wear the same pair of blue jeans every day for the whole week, and who would rarely, if ever, think to borrow one of their friend's pants, or shirts.

Girls, being more social in general, deal with their negative feelings about their peers by trying to isolate them, by shunning them, or by getting them shunned by others in their peer group. Some girls escape this pattern by making boys their primary friends. They are often seen as *"tomboys,"* because they react to situations more like boys would, and their interests follow more closely interests traditionally identified as boyish.

Boys, more typically, will have a higher boiling point before they take exception to something, but once identified it is likely to be dealt with more physically. After the physical confrontation, the situation may be seen as over, and they go back to being friends. In today's climate, issues do not get resolved, so they smolder. Animosities continue to be present over much longer periods of time today than they seem to have been in the past. Faculties, parents, and others want boys to solve their problems by talking them out, but they do not have an infrastructure supporting the request. Asking boys to work animosity out by discussing it typically does not work. So, the solution finds itself somewhere on the street.

It is not a criticism to point this out. It is one of the areas in life where the caretakers and teachers might help alter the continuing course of events. Children, who deal with their negative feelings by shunning their peers, become adults who will not talk to their mates when something goes wrong in the relationship. When, as children, we practice isolation techniques and we push people we think do not like us out of our lives, it becomes a habit we will likely continue into adulthood. Children who are unable to resolve conflict without physical confrontation become adults who turn to aggression or violence.

A second reason a girl may change best friends more frequently is that (tongue in cheek) they have better memories. I frequently see girls, ladies, women who seem to be able to recall the smallest slight they have received from someone years before. Perhaps it happens, but, if so, I have not experienced it very often in my boys and men. Freud is reported to have said one of the bases for neurosis was people remembering too much. It certainly seems to apply to this group of young ladies.

A third reason for this behavior actually applies to both boys and girls: this has to do with the early belief system of thinking *"others are responsible for my thoughts, feelings and actions; I am responsible for others thoughts, feelings and actions."* Because this is the point of view of children during the time when they are creating their first close bonds with others (parents, friends, boy and girlfriends), **it becomes the default**

system for individuals when they attempt to enter a relationship. This is especially important for adults.

This belief system **seems** to be **hardwired** (developmental) for the first twelve years of life, so it gets plenty of use. Let's look at this system in more detail.

This belief system generates products like hurt*, dissatisfaction*, disapproval*, jealousy*, waiting*, frustration* (anger), withdrawal* (suicide gestures,* suicide), resentment*, depression (depression generated from need for self, situation or others to be different from what the person wants*), intimacy problems, communication problems and a failure to develop a good sense of self (poor self-esteem). This list could go on to 75-90 items. (An * indicates behaviors identified as manipulative.)

Hurt* Where does psychological hurt come from? Typically it is when people feel slighted; when we do not see others as giving us our due; when we feel people are being mean to us through their speech or behavior. In other words, when we perceive others are causing us pain. Blame! Marcus Aurelius almost 2000 years ago said a person is only harmed to the degree they believe they have been harmed. Blame!

Dissatisfaction* and disapproval* are somewhat related in etiology. I am dissatisfied when something is not living up to my expectation, whether it is a behavior, or a person. If I am dissatisfied with them, I am also likely to show disapproval toward the person, or the event identified. Again, the sense is others are creating my negative experience. Blame!

Jealousy* is the feeling a person experiences when they have a sense someone they care about is interested, or is more interested, in someone else. Pathological jealousy is a psychiatric diagnosis. People who are jealous universally attempt to get the perceived cause of their jealousy (the other person) to accept the response-ability for their jealous feeling. Blame!

Waiting: The person reporting it, at times, does not recognize this feature, but if you listen carefully you will pick up the theme. *"I can't do that until my husband says it is ok." "I have to stay in the marriage until my children are out of the house." "I am going to get another job, as soon as my boss fires me."* Making others responsible for what comes next in our lives. Blame!

Frustration*: Frustration accompanies waiting. Do you like to wait? Not likely. Waiting contributes to the sense of frustration and helplessness. It is also the first level of anger. I tell my patients mild blaming causes frustration or irritability. Moderate levels of blaming cause anger. Severe blaming causes rage. This state of frustration leads in two directions. One is toward becoming angry and can end in violence, or murder. The other state leads to withdrawal, isolation and can end eventually in suicide. Which direction a person goes down is related to the individual's personality (Passive people tend to withdraw; assertive people tend to get violent) or to the personality of the people they are trying to manipulate. If the person being manipulated is aggressive the manipulator will more likely appear passive and vulnerable.

Helplessness*, Hopelessness* & Demoralizations* are progressions of each other.

Helplessness is, *"I cannot do it."* [We can blame self as well as others] *"I am not able to create a positive solution."* Hopelessness is when we see others as unable to resolve the issues, and demoralization is when we perceive no one can help us. The way people frame this issue is, *"I am hopeless because you do not help me."* Blame!

Resentment*: It follows if I believe you have the power to make me happy, and you do not make me happy, I will resent you. In a sense it is not much different from anger. If I resent you, I am angry with you for not doing what I think you should do- *"to make me happy."* Blame!

Depression & Sense of failure: These appear to be common products of the unsuccessful attempt to get others to change (do what we want). When I see poor self-esteem and many of the other products occurring along with depression, I have come to see the blame belief system as etiologic for these products. The sense of failure follows numerous unsuccessful attempts to correct the problem. Since blaming does not work, there is a constant string of failures. Blame!

All depression is not a product of biological/genetic factors. A feeling of depression can arise from needing self or others to be different. The perception is others create this feeling. Blame!

Communication Problems: How we communicate with each other is determined, certainly influenced, by our belief systems. Before I added this to the list of conditions, identifying the Blame System, I would ask patients, who seemed to clearly be in the Blame System, if they were inclined to tell people the truth, or did they tell others what they thought the person wanted to hear. Almost everyone, who sees himself, or herself, as causing other people's feelings, will tell me they commonly hedge what they say. They do not *"want to make others angry,"* or *"hurt their feelings."* This failure to be honest or direct in order to protect other's feelings is a communication distortion coming from blaming; in this case, seeing ourselves as responsible for other people's feelings. Blame!

There are several interpersonal dances commonly developed as a result of this communication problem. 1) Closeness→fear→screw-up. When one person (A) holds another (B) responsible for their (A's) feelings, it causes a sense of fear to occur as they get closer to each other. Typically when this happens one or the other in the relationship will do something, generally very stupid, to cause the relationship to go sour and pull apart. 2) Screw up→distancing→loneliness. After one party does something, both commonly go into a distancing process to protect them from further hurt. When people are in a Blame System, there are three ways they typically try to protect themselves: They create distance between themselves and others; they put up walls between themselves and others; and/or they turn off their feelings. Loneliness and isolation are the outcomes.

There is another factor making this problem even worse. After individuals go through this cycle of coming together→separating →incriminating, they, at some level, begin to understand they have a dependency problem. When this thought comes aboard there is an attempt to deal with the dependent feelings by becoming more independent. This is both a language and a perception problem. People think the opposite of dependency is independency. This is an incorrect understanding. The opposite of unhealthy dependency is a healthy dependency. When people try to deal with bad dependency by becoming more independent, it only leads to more isolation and loneliness. Unhealthy dependency has to do with needing others to provide something for us that we should provide for ourselves. Healthy dependency allows us to go to sleep in the same bed with another person and not fear for our life, or well being, and it allows us to get help when we need it.

Loneliness→narrowing the distance→chase→ vulner-ability. As loneliness builds people start trying to get back together again. If one person is ready, but the other is not, we get a chase. When the chaser closes in the vulnerability resumes and the process often repeats itself.

A psychologist has written a book in which he stresses for people to get close to each other, they have to learn to be vulnerable. This type of thinking is 180 degrees from my point of view, and I believe learning to be vulnerable is not only the unhealthy way to go, but it also contributes to people staying in System 1-the blame system. It is true if you are going to stay in System 1 Thinking you will need to learn to be vulnerable to experience closeness. The vulnerability comes from believing others cause our feelings. If one is going to stay in the Blame System, then learning to tolerate vulnerability is an appropriate (if misguided) endeavor to deal with something, which will never go away. When we understand others have no causal role in our feelings, there is no vulnerability, and we learn to do away with the defenses.

Intimacy is extremely difficult to achieve without direct communication. If I cannot tell you the truth, I do not really tell you anything of importance. Many affairs begin when one party starts talking with a stranger, because the person is a stranger, they do not see themselves as responsible for the person's feelings, so they have an open honest communication. They both agree the experience felt really good—so let's do it again! This works right up to the point when the two people begin to care about what the other one thinks of them, and then they change their communication style back to the old pattern.

<u>Failure to develop</u> a good sense of self comes from generating a feeling of constant failure. System one thinking generates failure because it is based in an attempt to get others to do what we think we need them to do for us to feel better. I estimate a 5 % success rate: my patients say the figure is far too optimistic.

<u>Developing a Poor Sense of Self is the outcome</u>. Compared to the problem of poor self-esteem, the other products of the Blame System are like the tip of an iceberg; the real damage is what this system does to self-esteem. When an individual spends 15-20 years, either assuming they are responsible for other's feelings, or being held responsible by others for their feelings, there is a warehouse of failures stored. These are at the heart of the *"sense of failure."*

Aggression is attributed to as many different causes as is suicide. The primary issues behind aggression are hormones, development, education, socialization, drugs and blaming. Most of the identified causes of aggression are actually just people, places, or events present at the same time the aggression is experienced. There is little doubt the male hormone testosterone contributes to the likelihood of aggression. Some girls manage to escalate to a high level of aggression even without this influence. Despite the role it plays, it is not causal of aggression.

Alcohol and other disinhibiting drugs can have a direct effect on the likelihood of aggression developing. My former karate instructor told how he would pick out a bar in different parts of the town to go to every month. Invariably, someone would pick a fight with him allowing him to practice his moves. Alcohol is a great disinhibitor. Children who are using alcohol and stimulants can be expected to be more irritable. This may be true also with prescription drugs. In my office, I do not use very many of the Dexedrine products when treating ADHD in children, because I see a higher incidence of irritability and moodiness with them. The same can occur with Ritalin products, but the incidence seems much less.

Studies show there is a greater difference between ring and index finger length in someone exposed to greater amounts of testosterone in the uterus. A relatively shorter index finger is associated with more aggression. This correlation does not hold for women.

As a group, boys and men are generally more aggressive than girls and women. There are exceptions, and certainly if an individual tries hard enough they can make a name for themselves in this area. Just above testosterone as a contributor for aggression lies a cause of aggression called blaming.

The cause of aggression is best divided into two forms. There is aggression related to predatory activities (theft, rape, bully behavior) which are intended to hurt others. These are acts by sociopaths or other unsavory individuals.

There is also **aggression related to inaccurate thinking**. The most common issues of aggression are related to the belief system <u>others are responsible for the way we feel</u>. If we do not feel happy, or content, we inaccurately see others as being the cause of our feelings, so we attribute our bad feelings to them. Since we see them as causing our feelings, we feel it is reasonable to attack them to get them to stop making us unhappy. Jails are full of people who claim they do not know why they are there. We smile and say to our selves, *"Oh, sure, it's a part of their con behavior."* In fact, many of them likely do not understand why they were put in jail. *"He was hurting my feelings; he was the one causing the problem; I just hit him to stop his assault on me. Why aren't you putting him in jail?"*

When we say something, we end up believing it; when we believe something we end up acting on the belief as if it is true.

There was a saying we had on the farm, *"people usually end up seeing what they look for."* When you look for disease as the cause of aggression you find it. If you look for blaming when you see anger, you will find it. The difference here is I do not give my patients a diagnosis and medicine; I give them information, so they get rid of the anger (without a diagnosis and frequently without medication). This is often true even when they have another diagnosable mental illness.

Inaccurate speech (beliefs) leads to an inappropriate behavior. This is the basis for nearly all childhood aggression. Children have a certainty others do cause their feelings; they have no awareness of mental intermediation, so they *logically* see others as causing what they are experiencing, and they want to get back at them to appease, or revenge, the feeling they are having. It is very difficult to convince children less than 12 years of age their thinking is not accurate. Younger children as a whole cannot see a difference between words being thrown at them and rocks being thrown at them. They deal with these events as if they were the same. To my knowledge, no one has tried to look at whether teaching children to speak more accurately would diminish these problems for the children; I know for a fact, it resolves a large amount of conflict in adulthood.

Anger is the feeling, and aggression is the behavior, in the non-predator type of aggression. Anger is created when we blame; anger is a product of blaming. It is common for people to think anger is related to an event, or action, generally created by someone else. This, unfortunately, is one of the many lies people tell themselves. Anger does not have any causal relationship to <u>events</u> preceding it, to comments people may have said, or behaviors they may have done. Blaming can have anyone, or anything, as its perceived origin, including self, or as in the case of psychiatry, a psychiatric diagnosis. The concept of <u>intelligent emotions</u> is a ship wreck; any evidence, to the contrary, still leaves anger as a waste of energy.

Non-predatory aggression is almost always a product of inaccurate thinking. Aggression comes from an error we make in the rules of our game of life and in the failure of our education system to correct this fundamental error in our thinking. It is another example of something present but generally unseen. Aggression, like anger, is a product of blaming, and blaming is a lie. Teachers/parents must begin to see they can help correct the developmental cognitive problem, as well as teach basics of math, history, spelling, etc.

Is aggression bipolar? As a psychiatrist, I can tell you all it takes to get a diagnosis of bipolar in my area of the country is to get angry. In approximately four out of every 10 new patients I see, anger is one of the chief complaints. Most of these individuals have been diagnosed with a bipolar disorder if they have seen a psychiatrist, psychologist or counselor. When people get this diagnosis they are frequently put on one or more mood stabilizers or antipsychotic medications. Article after article in the journals gives biological related reasons for anger. When I recently attempted to share my findings with a well-known Arizona researcher, I was dismissed with a one sentence written reply. If someone cannot make money with the concept it does not have much chance of surviving. I stand against the hurricane of current reasoning: aggression is rarely, if ever, a bipolar component. It may occur in those patients for the same reason it occurs in non-bipolar patients, but it is not a part of the disorder.

One of the basic tenants for a bipolar diagnosis is *". . . irritable mood . . ."* so everyone with a life has an entry to the diagnosis. **Irritability is caused by mild blaming; blaming causes anger; severe blaming causes rage**. I have seen many patients diagnosed bipolar for no other reason than having an anger problem. Anger can be gotten rid of when we stop blaming. Because it does not really require any of the forty-two medications recommended, it is something teachers can actually help to extinguish in children older than twelve. The attribute which should be correlated with bipolar is elation, which is different from irritability.

Blaming has probably killed more people than all the plagues put together.

Blaming is at the heart of the hatred for Americans, at the heart of the hatred for blacks, at the heart of the hatred for whites, for homosexuals, for the obese, for the intelligent, for the retarded—I hope you get the point. Mild blaming begets irritability, blaming begets anger and blaming superimposed on righteousness begets a fanatical, extremist type of insanity. Children unfortunately are often extremists in the perception they are correct. This fosters the radical side of issues. This can be corrected by using accurate speech.

Blaming is the process of attributing some form of cause for our negative experience to others, to events, or to a situation, when, in reality, the cause is mental intermediation. Failure to understand the mechanism and the importance of this mental intermediation leads to a misinterpretation of events. People see cause where none exists. Since teachers and parents frequently do not teach children how to make a distinction between cause and effect and sequential ordering of events in daily life, it is likely a person will make this mistake thousands of times in childhood.

[These concepts cannot be taught in just one day in a class assignment and then expect children to use them in their lives. They are issues needing to be addressed daily in children's lives-like good manners.]

Teachers/parents cannot teach what they do not know. It would be a simple matter for them to include teaching this in their curriculum, but since most teachers are also blind to the problems failure to expose this process can create, they cannot teach it, and, unfortunately, they often seem to promote the misunderstanding.

Blamers need to be right. They always have a high degree of belief they are right. This is because they spend so much time lying in one form or another, they do not know how to analyze situations for reasonable certainty. The serious reader needs to study non-sequitur and logic.

During a recent visit to Canada Pope Benedict XVI was critical of Canadians because of a dropping birth rate. In a world where more than half of the people go to bed hungry, where water is becoming a sparse commodity, and food is not readily available, advocating that it is negative to manage the rate of birth seems to me to be morally inept. This is actually an example of *post hoc fallacy.*

Let us look at another speech behavior: **arguments**. Arguments are almost always an attempt by one person to steal power from another person. If we need to be right, we try to badger the other person into giving in to our point of view. If we want to help the child, or other people, be able to navigate life better, we want to help them frame events in their life as accurately as possible. By teaching our grandson,

Andrew, to frame his experience accurately, it eliminated the conflict internally, as well as externally. To say he does not remember falling off the couch does not initiate an argument with grandmother. It is already an accurate statement, so there is no need to challenge it. He gets to be right; grandmother gets to be right. Both people are speaking correctly.

The purpose of argument is to cause the person you are arguing with to forget they have all the power in the first place. Think about it. If I know I can do what I want, why would I get into an argument with you about it? On the other hand, if I know you have all the power, and you can act on it the way you want, getting into an argument with you about it might cause you to forget you have all the power, and I might get my way. Never argue if you have the power, at the very best you can only come out of the argument with what you went in with, at worse, you will give away your power.

I will often review arguments with my patients and will ask, *"What was the argument about?"* Of the arguments patients tell me about, the ones in which they became the angriest, they almost always had all (100%) of the power to determine the outcome before they got into the argument.

The two major issues in life are not Freud's Oedipus complex and penis envy, they **are lying (dishonesty) and blaming**. In Sophocles' *Oedipus*, Oedipus did not want to kill his father and marry his mother as Freud suggested the average boy (child) desires; in fact, Oedipus found it so undesirable and repulsive, he blinded himself when he understood what he had done.

The tragedy in general is lying. The tragedy in Oedipus is everyone lied to him except the oracle. It was nice he was warned by the prophets that his destiny was to kill his father and marry his mother. He also needed to know who his real parents were if he had any chance at defeating the predictions. It is always difficult to act appropriate in any situation, if you only have part of the data you need.

The biggest lie is about truth itself; the lie is to say that truth can be known. I do not claim anything in this book is true. It may be as I see it, but I have awareness <u>the truth</u> is not an absolute, and it frequently shifts depending on who is in power over the subject at the moment. Our understanding of the truth is constantly in flux. Galen determined the direction of medicine for several hundred years before his science was discovered to be faulty.

J. Rufus Fears, in a Great Courses lecture by the Teaching Company entitled *History of Freedom*, takes a somewhat compelling position that truth is embedded in natural laws. This might work if there were any real agreement as to what really constituted natural laws.

Was the Native American's understanding of nature inferior, or superior, to what followed? The answer is a point of view, not the truth.

Knowing does not make it true. It was, I believe, either Will Rogers, or Samuel Clemens, who said the world was full of people who knew a great deal of fact that was not really true. Everyday we are confronted with this interface between science, reason, and belief. It appears Tom Cruise believes helping people through medicine is bad. I wonder if he will have this point of view if his appendix bursts.

Can we know anything for certain? Outside of specific areas the truth cannot be known. Mathematics may be one area where we take comfort in truths. 2 + 2 = 4. This is a definition with redundancy. It is only accurate if we pump in specifics making it true. 3 + 2 = 4 is not true. Why, because, we have defined it to be false. It has no truth of its own. If we wrote it another way it might be true: The food eaten by three small children + two adults= what four adults would eat.

Is the truth just what we want it to be? Violent television causes aggressive behaviors! Is this true or false? It may be correct in the incident where the child, or adult, attempts to act out a TV, or movie, scenario in real life and injures someone; it is not accurate for the majority of people who may actually rid themselves of aggressive thoughts while observing it played out in front of them in a fantasy medium. The factor not being considered is that mental intermediation by the person is what determines the outcome.

Individuals used to looking at data in a Baconian manner where facts are arrived at by a process of observation and verified by experimentation, know the problems related to establishing anything as fact. Hobbs said understanding is the faculty of perceiving the relationship between words and the objects for which they stand. Understanding is what someone can do with the facts. It may, or may not, be validated. If I study A. Beck, I learn something; if I apply what I learned, I can get a better understanding of what he was teaching, and, with time, I may even gain knowledge through using the teachings.

The sentence structure most readily getting people in trouble is the *"You made me . . . ."* It does not matter very much what follows the verb. The damage is done by the time the first two words are uttered. You might protest if the words after the *"You made me . . ."* are positive or nice it should not be a problem. The answer is it may not be a problem, but it is still generally inaccurate. Whether the sentence is *"you make me happy"* or *"you make me mad,"* it is still a distortion. It is not accurate speech as long as we are referring to events requiring mental intermediation before the conclusion is reached. If we are discussing a physical act, the word construction may be correct and useful. For example: *"He hurt my arm when he twisted it hard behind my back."* This describes a physical world behavior, and physical events are less subjective to the influences of mental intermediation. There are of course some gray areas. i.e.: Two children are playing. An event occurs. One child runs to mother and when he arrives he bursts into tears, *"Mommy, Johnny hurt my arm."* There appears to have been a lot of mental intermediation going on here; it does not rule out Johnny may have caused pain in the arm by twisting it.

As a part of the subject of communication, I would like to discuss predictions: *"You are going to fall. You are going to spill it. You are going to hurt yourself."* You probably recognize a number of these. There are many more.

Predictions have a way of not being very reliable. Usually, the person making this type of comment is expressing their fear something negative is going to happen to the object of their concern. The person typically wants safety for the person they are saying it to.

There are other predictions such as, *"You will never amount to anything."* This pattern of speech is mean. It is an attempt to hurt the person, or to belittle the recipient. These statements are like those declaring, if you do not do a specific thing, you will go to hell. These predictions are mean and manipulative.

Cautionary statements can be expressed as a concern, rather than a prediction. *"Please do not walk on the edge of the street, it is too close to traffic; I do not want to feel frightened, and I do not want anything to happen to you!"* This might take more words, but it conveys a real message the child can hear, and can learn to experience as true and reasonable. Predictions seldom come true, and if they do, they are accompanied by huge amounts of anger and guilt. Predictions lead to a sense, in the other person, of being lied to, and they fail to communicate the caring, or fear, they are intended to convey.

Predictions in day to day life are bad form, no matter how they are expressed. People are better off with honesty and accuracy, saying what they really mean, and doing the best they can. I believe stating predictions, as if they are the truth, is another way of lying, and it is another example of very poor, misleading, and inaccurate communication. Stating hundreds of times something is going to happen when it does not, fails to lead to a sense of confidence, or a sense of caring in the person hearing the comments. We want our children to believe us, and we may even want to tell our children the truth, but these types of comments lead a child to see adults as fallible and dishonest. It also has a second consequence; it leads people to think they can actually predict future events. Occasionally, something does come true. People will remember the one time they were correct, and they will not remember the 500 times they were not.

Transference is another mental activity poorly understood by teachers, parents and children. As used in psychiatry it means bringing feelings from an event in the past and attaching the feeling to a person, or situation, in the present. People can create transference issues just like they can create symptoms. Children do not understand this mental mechanism, and, therefore, they misinterpret the meaning of their emotional experience. In these areas, the teacher/parent has the option to teach children about this mechanism, only if they know about it themselves. Understanding this phenomenon gives the student the option to make an immediate difference in their life. Important here is the level of investment the student has in being right about their own emotional response. Teaching students about this type of thought, and the thought processing used in causing conflicts, can help to stop the creation of problems. A focus on transference distortions is a significant part of psychoanalytic treatment.

He who restrains his words has knowledge, and he who has a cool spirit is a man of understanding. Proverbs 17:27

Anger is created when we blame. People think anger is related to an event, or action, or disorder, generally created by someone else. This, unfortunately, is another lie people tell themselves.

Getting angry is like getting into your car, starting the engine, putting the gear in neutral and then pushing the gas peddle to the floor; it revs up the engine, but it does not move you forward.

If a teacher is working in the South, or in parts of the North, where a strong shame/honor culture (a society in which aggression is seen as the way to establish one's manhood) exists, there is a likelihood of experiencing more aggressive behavior among students and adults. Butler Field's book, *All God's Children* discuss this cultural finding. Studies have shown if one accidentally steps on someone's foot in the North the incident is generally quickly passed over and each party goes on their way; if this happened in the South, it is much more likely to lead to a physical altercation between the parties.

Blaming is what creates anger.

Anger is something teachers have to deal with. In today's society a lot of people who are angry are either put in jail, or are labeled bipolar. Neither of these end products is a good outcome. **Anger is a product of blaming.** As discussed before the first organizing belief system (others are responsible . . .) is a blame system, so it is commonly accompanied by anger problems. I have been unsuccessful talking children less than twelve years of age out of this belief system, and I am not certain whether it can be done. I expect if there were an organized effort to get children to speak correctly at a young age, it might be possible. This is an experiment I have not been able to do.

For children under the age of ten years it is generally best to take a behavioral approach to anger. You may tell them it is ok to feel angry, but it is not ok to hit people, or to destroy property when you are angry. Children do not cognitively understand cause and effect, but they do understand if they do X, Y will happen. This is a reasonable deterrent for the majority of children. This is also a good place to introduce Awareness cards. [Discussed shortly]

Blaming can have anyone, or anything, as its perceived origin, including self.

There is a lot of misunderstanding regarding emotions. Some teachers believe they should support whatever emotion children demonstrate. There is also a movement suggesting emotions are intelligent. I encourage a great deal of caution toward either of these points of view. The group who supports children's emotions, regardless of what they are, is generally attempting to be empathic. What is important to realize is when you respond empathically to any given emotion you may be putting your stamp of approval on that feeling. This means if a child is crying and you indicate you agree someone has <u>caused</u> the feeling of sadness, you have helped teach the child to keep this particular response to the event. What is less clear to people is that there is no one appropriate feeling to any event. The particular feeling generated is related to what the person tells him/herself about the event. The cop shows have it wrong.

Those who feel emotions are intelligent use arguments suggesting emotions like anger help to mobilize people to do what they need to do. Anger may be able to facilitate action, but if our thinking is working correctly, action should be based on reason, and not on emotion.

For children under ten to eleven years of age, the best approach is to teach accurate speech. It is harder to maintain an inaccurate belief system when people speak accurately. After the age of twelve, children can be taught to get out of the blame system and to get into a more self-accountable belief system. Before twelve they can be taught to express a situation correctly. In other words, they can be taught to speak accurately.

Anger does not have any <u>causal relationship</u> to events preceding it, or to statements people may have said or actions they have done.

Withdrawal is the opposite poll from aggression. If the opponent is seen as too powerful, or the person's own personality tends toward passivity, there is a likelihood they will respond to a perception of aggression from others by withdrawing. Sometimes the withdrawal may occur without others being a component. Children can withdraw from perceived threats even when no one else is aware there is a problem. What children imagine can be as real for them as any other reality. If a child thinks someone is going to be upset with them, it will reap the same outcome as if the person actually was upset with them. The more a child needs approval from someone else the stronger is their perception of what they think the other person may feel toward them.

The belief system, "*others are responsible for my thoughts, feelings, and actions; I am responsible for others thoughts, feelings and actions*" (System 1 Thinking) is like **the heads and tails of a coin**. At times a person will only see one side. It does not mean the second side does not exist. Generally, if you look you will see both sides of the belief affecting the person. It is not uncommon for people to tell me they do not hold themselves responsible for others thoughts, feelings or actions, but they will then go on to tell me how they do not communicate with others because, "*they do not want to make others unhappy.*"

The belief that we have the power to determine others feeling experience is just the flip side of feeling others determine our feelings. Either side of the belief causes problems. Understanding one side of the equation is not correct does not guarantee the pupil will still not believe the other side is accurate. It remains blaming regardless of which side is in force.

There are a lot of events adding coloring to a given problem, giving it some individual airs, but if this belief system is not addressed early in life, the time it takes to resolve a problem is greatly increased. This is a specific **mental intermediation**, or script, children and many adults adhere to it throughout their lives-with disastrous results.

Mental intermediation is about what our mind has to say. It is composed of the scripts we may be running in our life (Good guys never win ballgames; gays cannot make good soldiers) as well as the automatic thoughts going on in the background all the time we are awake. In order to understand our mind, or to help our mind help us to understand our feelings, actions, or thoughts, we must be able to reflect on what is in the mind; we must become aware of what is in our thinking.

The type of relationship we have with our parents can influence the way our mental intermediation is formed. I once saw a young lady who was having a really difficult time finding a boyfriend she thought cared for her. She had had a number of men who had tried, but she found them all wanting. Her complaint was having to tell them what she wanted. Not knowing what she needed, without her telling them, was a deal breaker for her. This became more understandable when she shared how her mother had taken her to see the doctor at the age of two years, because she had never cried. Mother thought there was something wrong with her. The doctor either pinched her, or gave her a swat on the bottom, and she cried. Mother had so completely anticipated her needs for the first two years of her life, she had never cried. What man is likely to replace mother in this scenario? Teachers can influence the way children process thoughts internally also.

You may be asking what you, as teachers/parent, can do about this developmental issue. The answer is **you can teach**. Parents also teach their children. It must be recognized that **teaching these principles is not the same as living them**. It is not enough to teach cause and effect relationships out of a book, it must be addressed whenever a child wrongfully uses the concept in the presence of a teacher/parent.

A mistake frequently made by parents/teachers when addressing these issues is to give the child a lot more of their time. A general rule is <u>children do what they do to get more attention from adults</u>; if what they do cause adults to spend more time with them, their behavior is reinforced, and it will become even more prevalent. Therefore, we need to be constantly aware as to whether we are reinforcing positive, or negative, behaviors.

This is a common dynamic in making problems worse. A child will misbehave and will be given additional attention; a child will hurt another child, and the child doing the hurting frequently gets the attention.

I am not against giving children attention; I am for giving children attention for those behaviors we want to have continued.

I devised what I call **Awareness Cards** to deal with these types of problems. These, as will become obvious, are not as workable, in their purest form, until children are able to write fairly well. The principal is an extinction model. You do not talk about the process at all, if possible.

On something like a 3X5 card you propose the following three questions:

1) What are you doing?
2) What is your behavior going to lead to?
3) What are your options?

It becomes the job of the student to answer the questions until the teacher is satisfied with the answers (the teacher can give the student as many cards as necessary, if the answers on the first ones are not satisfactory). It is not discussed at the time (**extinction model**). When the questions have been answered satisfactorily, the student can go back to the task they need to work on. The teacher can keep track of the cards for a given student and perhaps once a week for someone having a lot of trouble, or once a month for someone with only a few issues the cards can be brought out and discussed with the student.

They represent a behavior count as to the number of redirections the teacher has had to use with a child. It also pretty well addresses the type of issues being seen. It represents concrete behavioral evidence as to the problems the child is having, how they are experiencing the problems and whether they seem to be learning from the experience—and if it is kept in the extinction model, there is almost no time lost by the teacher in dealing with the child's behavior.

Intermittent reinforcements are actually stronger reinforcement of behavior than is a consistent reinforcement. Think of gambling. The occasional payout keeps people coming back, even when their overall experience is loss. If a student occasionally gets the payoff they want (spending more time with the teacher), it acts as a powerful reinforcement. It takes a lot of practice and awareness on the part of the teacher/parent to stay consistent and to not reinforce behaviors they do not want to continue. Almost all behaviors by children are reinforced by receiving more adult time.

Feelings are generated from several directions. One has to do with the interpretation of an event. The interpretation gives specificity to the feeling generated; the meaning of an event to the individual determines the approximate emotional response the person will manifest.

—I want to do everything right for people
  Love

—Everything is great
  Euphoria

—I like what is happening
  Happy

—My desires are being blocked
  Tension

—Happenings are not OK and are possibly dangerous
  Anxiety

—Situation is dangerous
    Fear

—I am less than I desire to be
    Shame

—I am unwilling to pay the price for my decisions
    Guilt

—I cannot accept where I am
    Unhappy

—I have lost something
    Sadness

—There is no happiness left
    Depression

—Negative assessment of one's direction in life
    Frustration

—Feeling of need to act on a perceived violation
    Anger

—Need for someone or something to be different
    Hurt

—Believing someone else is causing my negative experience

    Resentment

—I cannot do it alone and I have no support
    Helpless

—I have no expectation of success
    Hopeless

—Help is completely beyond reach
  Demoralization

Thoughts and feelings affect ones behavior; feelings and behavior affect thoughts; thoughts and behaviors affect the feelings we have. These three brain functions are what manifest our particular take on life. They are like the three primary colors, out of which all other colors (not quite true) can be created. And just like with colors, people do not always agree on what is primary. Some people are dichromatic, others may be tetrachromatic, but the majority is trichromatic. Just like shades of color people have shades of behavior, shades of feelings, and shades of thinking.

There is a second reason children, or adults, often do not understand why they feel the way they do. It has to do with a delay between when automatic thoughts occur and when the feelings, generated by those thoughts emerge. (Automatic thoughts are the background thoughts people have been running in their mind most of the time.) Because of a delay (15-30 minutes) between the thought and the feeling, people frequently do not recognize the relationship. A child may think their parents do not care about them; twenty or thirty minutes later they may feel unhappy and lethargic, or angry. Because, as mentioned, children are not good at understanding mental intermediation, or automatic thoughts, they do not see a relationship between those two events (their thoughts and the resulting feelings). I have to teach my adults to recognize these associations; it is certainly something we need to teach our children.

Our psychological feelings are a product of our thoughts and our actions. If I am in blame, the feeling will be anger. If I believe I am in danger, I may experience fear-unless I have the choice to be somewhere I feel safe.

Our physical feelings are also, often, a product of our behavior; if it is zero degrees outside and a person takes off their clothes and goes outside, they are likely to experience the cold. They are not going to get rid of the cold feeling by just deciding they want to be warm. If they could, it would be a demonstration of control. When asked why the person just described is feeling cold a lot of people will want to say because it is zero degrees outside; this is one way to look at the experience. It is where people focus who like to believe they have control. I prefer to see the experience of cold as coming from two choices the person made (after all the cold was there long before the person experienced cold): taking off their clothes, and going outside. Had they chosen to stay indoors they might not have gotten cold even if they had taken off their clothes; they might not have gotten cold if they had left on their clothes, or put on more clothes, even if they did go outside.

Major errors of childhood are 1) children are not aware there is **a psychological and a physical world** to learn about, 2) children do not realize the two worlds **operate by different principles**, 3) Children **learn** about the world around them almost entirely **by their interaction with the physical world**, 4) **children who are smarter often have even greater difficulty learning about the psychological world** because of their great affinity toward what they believe they have learned from the physical world.

The issue of physical and psychological addressed here is not the same old mind-body conflict which has been around for centuries—Descartes. It is not my wish to waste your time. What I would like, is for teachers to become aware there are words which better address physical phenomena, and there are words better addressing psychological phenomena. The power words in the psychological area are choice, selection and movement. The power words in the physical world are change and control. <u>**Using psychological words to deal with psychological problems speeds up the resolution of conflicts.**</u>

Another speech pattern needing to be watched for is related to the **concept of control**. People will use the word control to mean the ability to keep a car on the road (control the car by turning the steering wheel in various ways). This usage I have no problem with. Unfortunately, like the word responsibility which has two meanings, so does the word control. (This is another case of equivocation.) If we do not pay attention to which usage we have in mind, or which usage the person who hears it has in mind, it can cause a lot of errors in our thinking. I encourage teachers to make a distinction between language addressing physical and mental world concepts.

The **word control** has a connection to the **physical side** of the universe. Understanding this leads to different outcomes than when it is not understood.

One can take a board and work on it until it becomes a piece in the hull of a ship, or a part of the side, or floor, of a house, or a piece of art. These processes represent the first type of control, and it can be exerted over material elements. Materials can be made to fly in the air, dive into the ocean, or circle our planets.

In the second form of control, the meaning has to do with the power to make something do what it is not intending to do in accordance with nature. Let us take the comment *"you make me mad."* In this sentence, the person talking is attributing a power to the second person which they do not have. If we could actually *"make others mad"* we would possess an ability to go against the principles of nature. This would be an example of control of the second type. Since nature has not given one man *"control"* over other men's feelings, this form of speech is inaccurate. When people use this speech pattern, they come to believe the other person is actually making them mad, which is a failure to understand mental intermediation.

The word control is also used in this context: *"You should control your feelings." "My husband controls what I get to do."* This type of control also has problems. It is really more of an illusion than a reality. (Remember: When we say it, we come to believe it; when we believe it, we act as if it is true.) We really do not control our own feelings: mental or physical. In the psychological world we create them through our thinking process. Parents, teachers, and other adults sometimes think they are in control of the children around them; or they believe they should be able to control children. Children who are oppositional show them how this belief is inaccurate. Oppositional children may have more awareness that adults do not have as much control over their behavior as the adults would like them to believe. It would actually be wise for teachers/parents to thank their children for their good behavior:

it is recognition the child has responsibility and creativity over their behaviors. **Control is more of an <u>illusion</u> than a reality.** When we are in sync with nature, it appears we have control (events are going the way we want); when we want something against nature, we are likely to experience being out of control. This means the feeling of being out-of-control is essentially an artifact of believing one has control in the first place. **Change** and **control** are words and concepts grounding people in <u>physical</u> paradigm.

In **change,** we take something with a specific characteristic, and after we alter it, it has a different characteristic, form or use; pieces of wood become a desk; other materials are put together, and they become a television. In our speech, we are not very careful to choose words accurately reflecting what is going on. For example, we talk about changing the oil in our car, when what we are actually doing is replacing the old oil with new oil. If we could really change the oil, why not change it back to the way it was when we put it in the car in the first place, so we did not have to replace it. We also talk about changing our mind. How can we change something not having any physical attributes? What we more accurately do is put one idea to rest while we consider something else; it is the mind's equivalent of a movie camera. One picture replaces another in the mind's eye like it does in the camera's film. The picture frame last seen is not destroyed, it is not currently in the place to be seen. The picture may be viewed if the camera is played backwards, in the same way memories may come back into the frame to be recognized, if we look back on them.

Change has a paradigm meaning; it is associated with taking time, needing energy, using special information, and it is associated with stability and permanence. These are all physical world concepts. **This paradigm, when used to understand the psychological world, generates a belief that a lot of time is necessary to accomplish a task, more, or different, information is needed to accomplish the task, and it gives people a false impression the job is done when they experience the outcome they desire.** This belief system is why children, and adults, believe making a difference will be a long process for them. It is frequently the mental set behind children not believing me when I tell them they can create a different outcome immediately.

Children and their parents associate how long it took them to develop the problem, and how long they have been trying to solve/change the problem, with how long it will take to resolve a problem.

Children feel they are as smart as their teacher, parent, or the doctor, perhaps even smarter; they simply cannot/will not accept that these small adjustments in their thinking can create a different experience for them. However, such is the case. Is this faith, or knowledge, on my point? It is knowledge. For nearly 35 years I have had people report to me the differences this has made in their lives. It is a very low level abstraction concept. If you do it, you will see the effect.

Choice, selection and **movement** make the difference in the psychological world; and these actions can occur very rapidly. Furthermore, it takes no more energy to make one choice than another; it does not take any special knowledge (other than the awareness a choice exists); but the product is not stable.

In the psychological world, there is no change or control (unless you want to argue Mother Nature has control). Here everything exists all the time. The best way to think of this is to visualize a huge smorgasbord having all the options available to us lying there for the taking. When we take something up from the table and use it, there is a product produced, and it continues to be produced as long as we use a particular choice. Making a different set of choices creates new products. The original choices are not destroyed, they are simply replaced on the table, and they become available to choose again another time. This means there is consistency of product only if a given choice is continued over time.

The closest thing to stability in the psychological world is habit.

Children do not think about thinking; how the mind works is not on theirs. What is on their mind is how it hurts when you fall, or when someone hits you. They understand stubbing your toe is painful. They learn at an early age when something is too hard, too sharp, too loud, or too rancid, it is best to get away from it. In the physical world it is good to avoid what might hurt you. Because this is what children learn from the physical world, it is what they practice in both the physical and psychological world.

Unfortunately, when physical world principles are applied to the psychological world it creates problems; it leads to avoidance, and avoidance leads to many mental health issues. It also contributes to isolation, which in turn contributes to loneliness and alienation.

Do not use **avoidance** in the psychological world.

One piece of information needed to solve psychological problems is why it is not good, useful, healthy or helpful to avoid dealing with, thinking about or confronting unpleasant events in our lives. Avoidance makes these issues worse, not better; attempting to control (and/or change) our feelings is an unproductive way children/adults attempt to avoid what they consider disagreeable People are trying to create freedom from pain, when they *"push"* unwanted experiences out of their mind; pushing away memories of events leave the person susceptible to *"suppressed memories"* returning at some later date in their lives, usually when they want them even less than they did at the time of the initial avoidance.

There are two issues here. One is the early belief system already discussed. I also mentioned there are three frequently observed defensive maneuvers common to System 1 Thinking, which we use to ward off emotional pain: putting up walls and increasing emotional distance between ourselves and others, and turning off feelings. The second is the fact physical world lessons condition a person to avoid anything painful. The proof this approach does not work is the number of people in this system making suicide attempts, burning themselves, cutting themselves or withdrawing from life through items like drugs.

The belief system we want to replace the blame system with is, *"I am response-able for my own thoughts, feelings, and actions; others are response-able for their own thoughts, feelings and actions."* This belief system also pumps off products, but the products are much more helpful. This is what is referred to as System 2 Thinking (S2T). Accepting we are response-able for our own thoughts, feelings and actions is not a transfer of blame to ourselves as many children will initially perceive it.

In this belief system, we realize **need causes psychological pain** and **the antidote to need is acceptance.** When we move from need to want we get rid of about half of the discomfort we have, and when we move beyond needing to acceptance, psychological pain disappears. This is where we have the potential for happiness. There is no happiness on the need side of the issue. I tell people when they are in acceptance they are at the door of happiness: they still must go through the door.

When we accept we are creating our feelings we learn to act on issues more directly. An approach Dr. Emery (co-author of <u>Rapid Relief From Emotional Distress</u>) has suggested is the

ACT formula:

<u>A</u>ccept the reality of what is.
<u>C</u>hoose the options helpful in the situation.
<u>T</u>ake action on the choices you have determined to be appropriate.

When we accept, we are creating our own feelings, we experience the pragmatism of letting go of those concepts we have no ability to do anything about. People frequently add to their burden, because they keep carrying around problems they will never be able to solve. This is a waste of time and energy. Learning to put our efforts into what we have a chance to accomplish is a significant skill to learn.

In the blame system, we are focused on how to get others to do what we think we need them to, so we can feel good. Once there is an acceptance, we create our own experience, people start becoming more resourceful about finding solutions to their problems. These solutions are based on what the person does for themselves, rather than on attempts to get others to do what we think would help us feel better. The attack is an attempt to get others to be different, thinking it will change our feelings. It almost never does.

When people work on their own issues, there is a much higher success rate, and, therefore, a greater sense of success along with greater self-accountability. When people are in the blame system their focus is on others, or it is on what they need to do to get others to do what they think must occur before they can be happy. This is a very complicated and unrewarding endeavor.

Communication improves when people move into system two thinking. People in the blame system are not only blaming others for how they feel, but they also blame themselves for how others feel. Because of this, people will try not to tell others anything they think will be perceived as hurtful (unless they want to hurt someone else).

There are a variety of rites of passage in different cultures, or societies. Some of these are based on age, some on behavior. I would like to suggest teachers should be handing out badges to commemorate a child's consistent use of system 2 thinking over a period of several weeks to months. The awards could be handed out to youngsters above the age of ten who seem to function in the system most of the time, and could be given to those over twelve years who seem to persistently perform in the self accountability system.

Getting out of system one thinking is probably the most important cognitive developmental milestone occurring between the ages of ten and sixteen years of age, and it should be rewarded by recognition.

A spoke in this wheel of passage would include the successful identification and avoidance of inaccurate speech, the use of direct communication regarding desires and wants, achieving the ability to ignore ideas previously contributing to the person's negative feelings, identifying blame as a cause of anger and eliminating it.

When looking at the pain spectrum, we must break it down into smaller parts; the first division is between physical and mental. I am not discussing a backache someone has suggested to the patient is in his or her mind, but I am referring to the psychological pain related to depression, often to anxiety, to loss, and to life events in general.

There is pain associated with broken bones, inflamed joints, cuts, etc. Those are physical, and although a careful delineation can frequently find associated psychological issues, I am not discussing this set of circumstances now.

Pain = need. Psychological Pain can be considered as equivalent to need, or as a product of need. Either concept works.

The wife of a friend, a good therapist in her own right, and married to one of the best psychologists in Arizona, was on her way to her father's funeral when I asked if I could have a moment of her time. I said to her *"We are often caught up in the idea psychological pain is related to events, because it follows events in time (sequential ordering). If you can, in your grief, take a moment to remember pain is really a product of need (for something to be different than we believe it to be), and the antidote for need is acceptance, I believe you will have a less traumatic experience."*

She thanked me, and left for her father's funeral. When she returned, she looked me up. She thanked me for the comments I had made, and she told me she had pulled her mother aside and had spoken similar words to her. She felt they had both gone through the experience with much less trauma than either of them had thought possible. She seemed sincerely appreciative.

The next mental task, after determining if the pain is physical, or psychological, is to understand psychological pain is not caused by events, but is related only sequentially to events. Pain is a product of mental intermediation (needing self, situation or others to be different). Because this type of pain is not caused by events, it is important we learn how to separate our internal experience from external events. People who do not do this are on a constant roller coaster ride. The more clearly we understand we have a high level of manageability over the internal world, the better we can guide/direct our life experience. The less we understand this, and the more we tie our personal experience to the external world, the greater are the ups and downs in life. Some individuals, especially those inclined toward addiction problems, are known to be *"field dependent."* What this term suggests is that they are affected by physical world events more than is healthy.

Is pain, or *"not caring,"* the only options? Most people have had the experience of knowing someone who has had a tragedy, but it barely seemed to have fazed them; this reaction may lead others to label the person as cold or uncaring. Our investment in believing our own reactions are "exemplary" makes us certain no one could respond the way *"that person did,"* if they really cared; when their reaction is different from what we would have had, we think there is something wrong with their response. The confusion, again, is the belief that caring and pain are related. There is a Biblical story I recall attributed to King Solomon. He painfully grieved his son's illness while his son was alive, but when his son died, he arose and went back to work. People around him could not understand how he could behave as he did.

To get out of pain and to experience that it is optional requires recognizing psychological pain is due to mental intermediation. The specific thought process generating pain is a *need* for self, situation, or others to be different from what we believe to be true.

Others have had similar opinions: "A man is not hurt so much by what happens, as by his opinion of what happens." Montaigne

Belief is as powerful as reality. Note the "believe to be true" phrasing. Many times reality is already what we *"need"* it to be, but we just may not realize it; for example, I may want my wife to love me, but I do not feel she does; in reality, she may already love me. The feeling is generated not on the reality of the situation, but on what we "believe" the reality of the situation to be.

Needs lie on a spectrum from the true needs leading to death when not present (air, water, food, shelter, nurturance) to the trivial (a new dress or a VCR), to the state of acceptance, the condition of being out of need, which is the antidote.

$$\text{Need} \leftarrow \rightarrow \text{Want} \leftarrow \rightarrow \text{acceptance}$$
$$\text{(Pain)} \qquad\qquad\qquad \text{(No Pain)}$$

The stages of loss outlined by Elizabeth Kubler Ross point out the circuitous route people take when they do not go directly into acceptance. When people know what the task at hand is (getting to acceptance), they can go straight to the end point, and they can skip all the in-between.

The next important awareness is how it is possible to get rid of pain. Psychological pain is needing. We can get rid of need. How? Through acceptance, defined as grounding in the reality of what is and letting go of the need for it to be different. It is not resignation; it is not giving up; it is acceptance.

Some people are good at accepting; some people practice acceptance; others practice non-acceptance.

Another area important for teachers to understand is the issues related to **guilt and shame**. Because these two conditions often overlap, and they are frequently present at the same time in many conditions, it is easy to misunderstand them.

Guilt is the body feeling accruing when we are unwilling to pay the price for the decisions we make.

If a child is willing to be punished for something they have done, they will not demonstrate any remorse about the event. This tends to get adults concerned. Adults like to see children express remorse when they have behaviors the adults consider bad. There is a catch 22 here; those who are accepting responsibility for their actions will not be remorseful, and the ones who are showing remorse are the ones who are not being accountable for their actions. The adult correction's system actually penalizes those who accept accountability and responsibility for their acts while giving rewards to those who do not. As a teacher it is useful to understand this dynamic, so acceptance of consequences is rewarded, and failure to accept consequences is not rewarded. Guilt feelings may be extinguished by actively accepting the price, or consequences, related to the decisions we make.

Shame is different from guilt, but it may occur in the same event.

Shame is the body feeling accruing when our image of self and assessment of self do not match.

If a child believes they should be able to make everyone happy, but their teacher is not happy with them, they are likely to feel shame.

Getting rid of shame requires a different thinking process from getting rid of guilt. Where guilt is relieved by accepting the cost related to the decisions we are making, shame is not. To relieve shame the person must adjust either one, or both, of the following: assessment of self, or image of self. Our image of self is believed, according to psycho-analytic theory, to be started in the first couple years of life by taking into our mind (introjection) an idealized parent image (imago); not the actual parent's, but the idealized parent's persona. We add over the years all the should, ought, must, or have to, we accept for ourselves. This accumulation then becomes our image of self. This does not become an issue until, for some reason, we need to compare the image with an assessment of self. It is at this point a student will either experience harmony (good self-esteem) or disharmony (disparity between image and assessment). If the discrepancy between these two is a large one, they may experience a self-esteem crisis. This condition may be dangerous, and it is one of the points in time when children have been known to commit suicide.

Helping a child overcome a **self esteem crisis** can be as simple as helping them to turn down the intensity of the evaluating mechanism (the more critical a teacher or a parent is the more critical the child is likely to be about themselves) so it is less critical. The other option is to help the child get rid of specific images they should have thrown away. It is like going in and cleaning out our bedroom closet. Most people hang on to belongings they should have gotten rid of a long time in the past. This is true of our image of self. If we have unrealistic expectations, it is time to get rid of them. Believing we should be able to please <u>everyone,</u> for instance, is impractical. It is not always possible to please even one certain person.

When we can clean out the unreasonable expectations, and can look at ourselves with a reasonable amount of criticalness, we have an excellent chance of achieving noteworthy self esteem. The other factor creating poor self esteem is system-one-thinking which prevents the development of a good sense of self.

Contributing to the issues of shame and guilt are the **automatic thoughts** children develop based on their experience with the world. If a child has had a good or beneficial experience with living, they are more likely to bring positive thoughts with them. If, on the other hand, they have had a lot of negative, or painful, experiences, it is likely their automatic thoughts will run toward the dark side. A child who is fearful, or avoidant, may have been injured, but this is not always the case. It is important to remember in many cases the belief we have been injured may be as much of a problem as a real injury. A teacher's willingness to listen to the child's issues can be very helpful.

Guilt, in a practical sense, has nothing whatsoever to do with the rightness, wrongness, goodness or badness of any given act. It is purely the end product of the way an individual perceives his action. All decisions should be composed of at least three parts (ACT formula): The first is an evaluation (Assessment) of the alternatives, the second is a consideration of the costs and rewards (Choices available) a given action will bring, and the third is action (Take Action). There is no decision (only action) when individuals are unwilling or unable to evaluate the costs. When we act without assessment a much higher rate of guilt feelings arise from our day to day "actions." Example: An individual, who goes to Las Vegas and places money on the spin of a roulette wheel, will feel guilty only if he cannot afford the loss, whereas an individual recognizing and accepting the possibility of loss will not be as devastated as a person unprepared psychologically to accept the possibility of loss. (He may be just as broke, however.) Costs are not all measured in money; a teacher's disapproval, a peer's harassment, a principal's displeasure all represents potential costs in making decisions. An individual not considering costs is setting themselves up to develop guilt. Eliminating the experience of guilt requires learning to evaluate carefully what the potential costs are in any decision and to see if the psychological attitude to accept the costs is present. Students may be advised if they cannot afford the costs of a given decision, then they should make another decision. Example: If one cannot afford to fail, perhaps one should make time to do the homework.

The mechanisms creating these two states are quite different. Helping a person deal with these two experiences requires a few moments to elicit which condition the individual is discussing. Even though the two may be co-mingled and may exist at the same time in a given individual, one must help them divide their experience into the two parts, so they can apply the proper principle to bring about a solution. Past experiences of guilt will still respond to "acceptance-of-the-cost related to the decision made," as will current experiences. If a person does not want guilt to appear in the first place, they must assess and then choose to accept the costs before taking action. Shame responds to balancing image and assessment; guilt does not.

"Guilt upon the conscience, like rust upon iron, both defiles and consumes it, gnawing and creeping into it, as that does which at least eats out the very heart and substance of the metal." South

"I never wonder to see men wicked, but I often wonder to see them not ashamed." Swift

Students often carry their own visions of **shame and guilt**. For most, guilt is the feeling they have when they believe they have done something wrong and are possibly going to be punished, or they have evoked someone's displeasure. Shame, a less frequently used description of oneself, is the term conveying exposure of our faults to others. In the past, shame was often tied to exposure of some body part to another. In some societies today it is shameful for someone to see your face. Exposing an ankle was, at one time, a disgrace. Traditionally shame and guilt have important psychological differentiations. This should be kept in mind by the teachers if they are going to understand children's communications. Students, being unaware shame and guilt describe different personal experiences, do not use these terms clearly.

Most developmental researchers agree shame and guilt emerge somewhere between the ages of two and five.

The experience of shame is usually an episodic event. It occurs when the individual compares a minds-snapshot of where they think they <u>are</u> to a mind-picture of where the person thinks they <u>should be</u>. When these pictures can be superimposed on one another, there is harmony and no shame. When the current snapshot is seen as better than expected we have a sense of pride. When it is less than expected we have a sense of shame. If the disparity is too great we have a self-esteem crisis.

Perfectionists have a tendency to try and work themselves out of these perceived crises by doing more, but this does not help, because one can either be in harmony, or in crisis, at any point on the axis of performance. The only way to experience less shame is to bring the two pictures (assessment of self and image of self) closer to being superimposed on one another.

This can be done in two ways: one, we can adjust downward the image of what-we-should-be, and, two, we have an option to get rid of some of the should, ought, must, and have to concepts. Perhaps I can settle for pleasing others 80% of the time instead or 100% of the time. The more critical I am when I look at the snapshot of my current level of functioning, the larger the disparity I will see. If my parents were very critical, it is likely I may continue criticalness into my own assessments, but this can be adjusted down to allow the images to come closer to each other. Where an individual believes he should be functioning is relative, and many who function at an extremely high level still experience disharmony, because their perfectionism leaves them feeling they are not accomplishing what they should.

When a person experiences a need to be perfect, which is why they are called perfectionists, it results in a sense of shame about day-to-day failures, and these individuals, unable to raise their behavior to the level wanted, will experience a sense of disharmony. Helping some people over this sense of shame can simply mean raising, or improving, their level of functioning, as in helping a student understand a math concept, so they can do better on tests, thereby better matching the image they have of themselves; or helping may require lowering their image, or expectation, so it more closely matches their capabilities, as when a child with an I.Q. of 80, might find more success as an animal trainer than as a graphics designer. Sometimes in the clinical setting, I have to help parents lower their expectations, so the child is not getting a constant sense of disappointment about their performance from the parents.

A developmental task occurring between the ages of 10-12.5 years is for the child to **learn how to ignore those behaviors of others they feel are contributing to their being upset**. When children are able to do this, it puts them on a good path for a healthy adulthood. The ability to separate events and feelings appears to be critical to developing accurate thinking; learning to ignore what is seen as causal to the child's feelings is crucial to their getting out of the blame system. Learning this creates a small period of time between an event and the feeling associated with the event. This allows the child to see and to understand there is no direct connection between their wants and their feelings. When children are able to do this fewer misunderstandings develop.

Children, before the age 10-12 years, are locked in a belief system, true for them, but not accurate. "*You (others) are responsible for my thoughts feelings and actions, and I am responsible for your thoughts, feelings, and actions*" leads to a way of processing events children will hopefully get away from by 12.5 years of age.

When unpleasant experiences happen to children between birth to 12 years of age, the child has no choice in the way they assess the experience. So, depending on what their experiences are, children come into maturity with good and bad memory deposits. The more conflicting, painful, and erratic a child's life is, the more certain they are that others are responsible for their feelings, thoughts and behaviors. The more unhappiness they bank, the greater is the investment they have in their perception being true. If I have been told all of my youth Americans or Jews are bad people, at 25 years of age I may perceive it is my duty to become a human bomb and destroy them. The child who cannot accurately discern *cause and effect* from *sequential ordering of events* will have no mechanism by which to evaluate, or reason through the correctness, or bias, of what he/she has been taught.

Trauma in childhood is behind the problems we see in a group of psychiatric patients called "borderlines." These individuals have had the misfortune of banking many negative experiences as they are growing up. Their investment in their belief about the world (System 1 Thinking) is immense. As adults they often seem to have the ability to understand the principles of S2T, but they are unable to put the awareness into action. As adults, they will tell me they understand their children are not responsible for their getting angry, and one minute later they are yelling at the child "for making me mad."

Persistent and negative input can affect how a person responds to stress. A consistent stress can eventually affect the way a person feels. Stressors are generally not causal of actions. A child who endures years of physical and/or psychological duress is certainly going to be affected by those events. From the child's perspective if they pick up a gun and shoot someone, it is the other person's fault. (System 1 Thinking) There may be a lot of contributing issues here (being bullied), but this does not cause the person's actions. The child, however, does not see, or experience the event in this manner. As a society we need to understand children do not process information in the same way healthy adults can.

Where does causality lie in the case referred to above? Perhaps in the failure to be taught how to solve or resolve problems non-violently, maybe in a social system failing to provide clear options for children in intolerable situations, or in the laws indifferent toward the struggle of individuals until an event has occurred. Each, or all, of these failures could cause a change in the form the outcome takes. A person in a degrading non-consensual situation needs to understand there are viable options available to them. People seldom do better than their best awareness allows, however.

In life, as well as in medicine, we have an attitude, we should not do anything until a problem manifests. In medicine this means too little time is spent in prevention; in law, it means we feel we need to wait until a crime has been committed before we can do something. There is a black and white aspect to waiting until a disease is present, or a crime has been committed. This is a major complication. This falls right in with throwing all the evidence out, because someone did not collect it according to some arbitrary set of rules made up by someone who does not have a finger on the pulse of sanity.

A dynamic children do not understand very well is how **someone's unhappiness with them** can progress to their working for the person. It is generally nice when people like us and want to please us, but this can become a living nightmare when it goes too far. Whether it is related to the boy wanting the girl to like him, the girl wanting the boy to like her, or the child wanting the teacher or the parent to like them, it is important for the child to understand how needing to have others like us can turn us into servants. Some children try too hard to get others to like them. I see children who will try to buy (with gifts, food, and even money) other's friendship. It would be helpful if children were taught about this interpersonal dynamic.

Lying can be a problem for some children. Looking at moral development in children has uncovered some surprising and, at times, unsettling findings. For example, stealing may be more a product of opportunity than of any absence of proper teaching. Because of these types of findings, it may be wise to deal with lying and stealing with logical consequences rather than with moralistic approaches ("That is bad"). I suggest when children have discovered lying, adults can/should choose not to believe anything the children tell them. This may sound severe, but it often disrupts the behavior very quickly. The way this works is the parents agree to anything the child wants, but at the time of execution they renege, telling the child, *"Oh. I am sorry. I did not know you actually wanted to do that, I just thought you were lying to me."* Children really hate this, and typically the lying stops very quickly. This may not be practical in the classroom.

Teachers should make the practical assumption, if the child is not turning in homework they are lying to the parents about not having homework. This can be addressed by notifying the parent directly (phone, e-mail) if the child has homework.

[Children with ADHD often do not turn in homework even when they have completed it. This is one of the last features of ADHD to disappear, even with a super response to treatment. It is not helpful for the teacher to assume the stance that it is the child's responsibility to get their work turned in and then to leave the issue there. This problem is a part of the larger medical problem—ADHD. In order for the child to get his/her work turned in there frequently needs to be a handoff procedure in place between the teacher and the parent.]

Lying is an interesting problem in childhood; it is also a complex matter to deal with. People (especially parents) have a lot of negative feelings about children lying, yet they often do not see the many times they will lie to a child. It is so complex; I am having trouble formulating it here. Let me try to explain some of the ways we lie.

Othello's destruction came about from the lies of Iago. This was a type of lying intending to destroy another person. One of man's favorite past-times appears to be lying. It is interesting how many of the children I see in my office who go through a period of lying behavior. Lying really bothers parents. They can get quite upset about it. Children often lie to decrease their homework or to get more time to play. They lie about circumstances they want to be true (*"I do not have any home work."*)

What about the lies of adults? Some lying is malicious and with intent to destroy (Iago), but the vast amount of lying in adulthood seems to be in gray areas.

From Santa Claus to the tooth fairy, parents encourage the acceptance of a lie by their children. It is good for commerce, so it is acceptable. We lie almost every time we tell a child to "Sit *down, or you will fall.*" It is a lie in court when judges ask people to tell the truth, the whole truth, and nothing but the truth, and then make certain they cannot. These are lies people not only accept, but often they help foster. It is like we have an unconscious accounting system saying, *"This lie is ok, but another lie is not."*

Most of the deeds we attribute to others throughout a day are not accurate. *"You make me happy; you make me sad; you hurt my feelings; you make me hate you; you made me love you; you made me buy the dress; you made me stay at home; you made me think this way."* All are lies. We tell these lies to ourselves, and we tell them to others. We make songs espousing these ideas; we write books and make movies based on the lies. There is no shortage of people promoting these lies, but there is a shortage of people who understand they are lies. Possibly, one of the biggest lies we hear all the time is *"It is for your own good."*

Because of this duplicity, the issue takes on a very high level of abstraction in people's minds, and when abstraction is high there is little agreement among people as to what is correct. Acceptance of this duplicity creates a general attitude that if I see it as alright, then it is not a lie. [*"I did not have sex with that woman."*]

Blaming is a lie. Blame language is generally not accurate speech either. It is not accurate in daily life, and it is not accurate in the courtroom. Blame is a lie many conspire to maintain.

There is power in knowing if what we are told is accurate. The ability to see into a situation and know if what is being said is true, or not, is paramount. In our society, where lying is such a huge part of how we communicate, we generally do not like those people who can see through our lies. One group of people who commonly confront us about our lying is our children.

Parents will say to a child:

> *"You cannot go outside until you finish your homework!"*
> *"You cannot play ball in the street."*
> *"You must take your medicine every day."*
> *"You cannot ride your bike in the street."*

The child sees right through these statements. They will often, immediately, go out and do whatever they were told they could not do. Why? Well, one reason is because they see through the lie; they are aware they have the ability to do it, so they just do it. The compliant child, on the other hand, may believe the lies. The third option is the child knows it is a lie, but chooses to go along with the command anyway, usually to please the parent. Why are these lies you may ask? Because, they are really directives the parent wants the child to accept, but they are expressed as if the parent has the power, when they actually do not have the power. Children, often, take some pride in having the power to defy an adult. I have seen children who would provoke a spanking from a parent just to have the satisfaction of experiencing their perceived power over the parent. When parents feel their children *"make them angry,"* they are essentially giving the child a huge sense of power.

Why do we keep telling lies? One reason is we grow up with them. Lying is what everyone does. We are just trying to fit in.

What do we need to do? Practice speaking accurately. I suggest we put more energy into understanding our language and telling fewer lies. It begins simply with telling our children something like, *"Please get down from the rail; it would hurt if you fell, and I get anxious when you do that."* Or you could say simply, *"I get anxious when you do that, please stop."* or *"I fear for you when you do that, please stop."* The *"Get down, you're going to fall,"* is harsh, it is likely not truthful, and it does not convey you are anxious about their well-being, or you care about them. Statements of concern are truer; a statement of concern is a message meaning something different to the child. *"I know of children who have been hurt playing in the streets, so I am not comfortable when you do that. I know you are skilled and do not see it as a danger, but I would appreciate your not doing it. I want you to be safe."* It takes a few more words, but it expresses the real issue a command, or demand, does not express?

To help children, adults must become aware of the lies we all tell. When adults, or children, tell someone they have *"pissed me off,"* they are lying. When you tell a child, husband or wife they are *"making you mad,"* you are lying. We may not be able to wake up the courts to these facts, but we can become more alert ourselves, and we can take the knowledge as jury members into the court process, as teachers into the classroom and as parents into the home. If we, the jury, will not play the game, the courts will have to do something different. If women stop playing into the lies following them for thousands of years (women defile men), the social system will have to make another choice. Children lie; adults lie; nations lie.

We need to be careful when we attribute cause and effect, or cause, to an event or situation. A story line appearing in movies is where the bad guy has the good guy's friend, and he is telling the good guy how it will be his, the good guy's fault, if the friend is killed by him, the bad guy. Attorneys must have created these situations. This story line usually gets twice as many people killed. I guess it is a type of blackmail, or terrorism, which we are supposed to pay off to resolve. It is a distorted type of thinking.

Stealing can be more difficult to deal with depending on the support of administration and family. Children who steal should understand such behavior loses them the right to privacy. Children who steal need to have their belongings searched periodically. It just makes sense. Privacy is an earned status for children; it is not an automatic given. This may be a problem implementing in the schoolroom, but it should be the order of business in the home.

A difficult but related area is the issue of "What is right?" People do not like to accept that they do not know what is correct. What is right is a high level abstraction concept, and there might be little consensus about it; yet people will go to the extremist level to assert their point of view is the correct one.

Children have an extensive investment in the concept of being right. The investment in being right contributes greatly to the misery mankind experiences. This problem ties in with the need to speak correctly. When we frame speech in the "this is the way it really is" form, we are back to high level abstraction concepts and lots of disagreements about what is best, true, or right. The low consensus contributes to the desire to be argumentative about the issue. Selling our point of view about what is right is big business.

Teaching more accurate responses helps to frame issues more accurately and therefore it can, at least theoretically, reduce the amount of conflict in a situation. *"I believe X is true, is different from "X is true."*

People are not good at expressing situations or conditions accurately. Children can learn to accept a person who needs to be right, without accepting what the person adheres to as correct. One of the most important and difficult concepts I have to teach patients in my office is to learn to accept others where they need to be. We do not have to accept what they believe, or what they want us to believe, but at the same time we need to be able to accept another person where they need to be. Not doing this is the road to extremism. Most children less than 12 years of age are not very amenable to this concept. Teaching accurate speech might be a help even to the younger members of society.

The mental health implication here is how **the need to be right** creates problems in the person with the need, and it creates more problems for anyone they attempt to force to accept their concept of right. Rather than going into the thousands of examples of this in daily life, I am going to suggest what may be the best approach from a mental health perspective.

Since no one really has a corner on what is right, and what is right is not a provable condition most of the time, there is no particular reason we should be offended by anyone's point of view about life different from our own—as long as they do not force their point of view on us. Having a point of view has not yet been relegated as against the law in the United States, although it has been proposed by certain countries in the UN.

So, with an issue having this much potential steam behind it, how can a teacher weave through all the likely problems in this area? I think a focus on speech patterns is the most appropriate approach. When children, or adults, make dogmatic statements it creates the desire to challenge them. When we frame our experience, in *"I feel,"* or *"I believe,"* there is less tendency to provoke conflict. As a general rule we need to be aware even science does not reveal the truth, it only shows what was in a particular circumstance. {When scientists first detonated the atomic bomb, there were those who thought the explosion might create a chain reaction catching the atmosphere on fire and burning up the entire world. Fortunately, it did not happen.}

Dishonesty by omission (withholding the truth) **or commission** (telling an untruth) is a common by-product of the blame system.

Children will not tell the truth because they want to control the outcome. Adrienne Rich, in her book *On Lies, Secrets and Silence*, says the issue in lying has to do with a concern about losing control. Children love to steal power from adults, and they get a sense of power and control when they successfully lie to others. One of my high school contemporaries liked to confuse our English teacher Mrs. Kimbrough by telling her she did not really give us the assignment she knew she had.

If others' displeasure *can make you feel bad*, you feel you have to tell them what they want to hear. Lying becomes the only option for *making others feel good*. When you fail to tell the truth, minor issues escalate into major ones. When they believe the truth will hurt others, children reserve honesty as a last ditch defensive weapon. The solution, of course, is to say what is accurate, and to let the chips fall where they will.

We can help children understand **other's inconsistencies**.

In therapy, there are often questions related to why people do what they do. Why does a boy say he loves you, but then he never calls back? One way I try to help children understand this behavior is to look at the person we are trying to understand as having three internal factors influencing their decisions: thoughts, feelings, and actions. Each of these has an influence on the other two. One's actions will influence their feelings and thoughts; their feelings will influence their thoughts and actions; and their thoughts will affect their actions and feelings. We have <u>internal consistency</u> when thoughts, actions, and feelings are in concert with each other and are all pulling in the same direction. When what we say we want is followed by a behavior going in a different direction, it is highly suspected there are feeling issues interfering with the outcome. This creates the preverbal spinning of the wheels, a condition which may cover a lot of ground, but does not get us anywhere. It is like driving around in a cul-de-sac. This constitutes a condition of <u>internal inconsistencies</u>. This explanation sometimes helps children understand better whether father is lying, or not, when he tells them he will call them, but he does not.

If a person says he feels he is in love with a girl, but he cannot act in concordance with what is said—like buying her flowers, or calling her again for a date—it does not necessarily mean he is lying; it may just mean he is not internally consistent. Consistency should become the default position with time. In other words, we ought to get more consistent in our actions over time. This is not the case with people who are sociopaths.

What is the most important thing I can tell you about living a successful life? I would have to say it is the ability to keep a separation between our inner self and the activities going on around us. I see an endless line of patients attributing their depression, unhappiness, success, failure, anxiety, and etc. to what goes on in the world around them. When I ask a person why they think they are depressed and unhappy, and they make comments like, *"my brother-in-law has cancer, my uncle lost his job, my mother is getting Alzheimer's,"* I know they are not doing a good job separating inner experience and outer experiences. We need to be aware of the external world, its resources and its limitations, but what we do not want to do is to attach our sense of well being to the outer world. The outside world is in constant flux: your boss may love you today and tomorrow may fire you; your boyfriend may lament his love for you tonight and never call you again. The more we connect our inner life to the external forces around us the more chaotic our life becomes. Examples of well known people who have mastered this art are Gandhi, Jesus *("Forgive them father, for they know not what they do.")*, and Stephen Hawking. Many people are able to do this, but unfortunately, too many do not. The world we have a potential to stabilize is the internal world, and it can only be stabilized if we stay disconnected emotionally from the external world. This is not isolationist talk. We need to try and understand the best ways to interact with the outside world—we need to recognize we are separate from it. The only legitimate power we have is the power over our own thoughts, feelings, and actions.

Teachers teach what sentence structures do not make sense, but are they teaching what sentences do not make sense? **I see teachers in a key position to improve the world's mental health.** Perhaps they have already changed the world of individuals, but this is not what I am referring to here. Teachers have an opportunity to teach ways of making sense out of the world which they are not doing at this time. My teachers helped me accumulate a lot of information, but I was in medical school before someone taught me something I thought was critical. I remember a talk by the head of the Department of Medicine at the University of St. Louis. It has always stuck with me. He said he might not be able to teach us everything we needed to know about medicine, but by the time we left, we should be able to understand how to solve a medical problem. He was stressing process over the content. I also recall when I was in high school how much I hated history, now I can hardly get enough on all levels; in school, I had to remember specifics, but now I get to review it for process. What teachers do best is teach, we should let you, but you not only need to teach math, English, literature, history, etc. you need to teach some fundamentals about life. Will this ever happen? A lot of people will continue to work to make certain it never happens. Just like judges make certain juries never get all the information.

These additional fundamentals should be taught:

- Speech is a behavior: When we say it, we are going to believe it; if we believe it, we are going to act as if it is true.
- What we think we know to be true as children may not be true as adults.
- Failure to be flexible enough to accept a different understanding, when the time arrives, locks us into a non-working system. (Blame System)
- Learning to speak accurately is critical to a healthy life. (Teachers now focus on whether we speak correctly.)
- Truth is obtainable only as an idea.
- Repeating the same behavior, or thought process, over and over expecting a different outcome is a good definition of insanity.
- Control is a word best used to deal with physical world interactions.
- Choice, selection and movement are the power words in the psychological world.
- Whether it is *"true"* there is a mental and physical world or not, we still need to be aware there are languages referring to each of

these worlds. Sometimes a single word has a different meaning depending on which word one is referencing.

- It is imperative we understand the difference between cause and effect and sequential ordering of events, **and that we use and practice the knowledge**.
- Our feelings are not caused by preceding events, but by mental intermediation.
- We live in a world better understood as a *creation world* than as a *change world*.

Current speech patterns predict future behavior. Blaming is one of the primary speech patterns creating behavioral problems. If teachers do not address blaming in the school while children are still in the learning model, it is addressed later at home usually as a right and wrong issue. Children have a propensity to struggle with parents over those issues; in the opposite vein, they often blindly follow what their teachers tell them without question. In the hospital setting, I would use this awareness, and when I wanted a child to learn a specific principal, or to get a different perspective on how to solve a problem they were having, I would ask the teacher to work the concept into one of their assignments. When I asked the child what they were learning in school the next day, they would teach me, usually with excitement, what I had wanted them to learn.

What I am suggesting is that teachers have an opportunity to teach children about S2T as a part of their learning. It is crucial for children to understand the process of their thinking (their operating system) as it is not accurate (System 1 Thinking); they will have a better ability to understand why their thinking is this way after the age of twelve. I would go so far as to say there should be a badge of recognition earned by the child as soon as it is clear they are using S2T in their daily living. It is truly the dividing line between being a child and being an adult on a mental grid. Children are not as willing to learn responsibility and accountability issues from parents as they are from teachers. Parents spend way too much time telling children what to do, rather than helping them to learn what works. Parents can be perceived by their children also as teachers, but they frequently are not.

Children can learn realities about their world, which go against their perceptions, but it is difficult for them to do this when outside the school setting. I remember learning color is not an attribute of the item observed, a challenge to all of my perceptive skills, but I could accept it because I was in an academic setting when I heard it. I might, or might not have accepted it if my mother had tried to explain it to me.

Empathy is another communication issue. It is useful to establish an empathetic relationship with others. The problem with being empathic, as it is usually done in life and in therapy, is it helps the person accept their misery. When a therapist takes a position *"If that happened to me, I would feel the same way,"* or *"I feel like you do,"* essentially, what is being said to the person is that what they are experiencing is the accepted norm. Even if I believed it, which I usually do not, I would rarely indicate to a patient what he/she is feeling is correct, unless, for some reason, I want them to continue the feeling.

There is no one right way to feel about most events. Cop shows have it wrong. If what someone is feeling is the right way to feel, then how can you help someone feel differently? When someone comes to see a psychiatrist it is usually not with the intent to continue feeling the same way. When I hear people's intensely sorrowful stories, I say something like, *"I am sorry you are having this experience, would you like me to help you get rid of your pain?"* When this comes in the first 4-5 minutes of an initial treatment session, some people are surprised and some are pleased, but most people want me to help them. My empathic position is that I do not like to be in pain, maybe you do not like to be in pain, if you agree, let us do something about it. It is helpful to anticipate what the mental intermediation is likely to be.

Needing is different from loving. When people have experienced a severe trauma like losing a child, one should be cautious not to validate the painful feelings—even the reasonable and understandable ones. This is not what people who want to let go of pain need to hear, they already know it. They can learn loving and pain are two different emotions, and you can give up one (pain) and not take anything away from the second (loving).

As I said, my empathic position is I do not care for pain, so I want to get rid of pain now, rather than later. Are you interested in my help? There is little doubt in my mind this is an empathic position; the problem is in the individual's limited awareness as to what is possible and the level of their willingness to make different choices.

Children generally do not trust others. They are lied to so many times in childhood it is difficult for them to believe what people tell them about life. Because of this distrust, they rely on their own experiences first. When our experiences in life do not reflect what people are telling us, it leads to distrust.

Assessment is an ongoing process. We need to teach, or be taught, the process of communication and negotiation. *"Son, if you do not come when I call you, not only will I be concerned about where you are, but I will have to charge you something for your behavior. You will not like the charge. I do not have to charge you for your negative behavior, but since I can, I probably will."* Or *"Son, if you refuse to come when I call you, you will likely miss out on a lot of goings-on you would enjoy like dinner or shows."*

We all too frequently want to force outcomes to happen. Children can be confused about requests. They do not understand the reason for certain requests, or actions, by adults. If they do not understand the nature of a request, how can they be expected to think through and come up with the most helpful action to a request? Our child rearing practices reflect our politics: we (the people) want to be able to tell the rest of the world what to do; we do not want to negotiate. We want to force events to happen, and we want them to happen our way.

Assertiveness training is one of the mental health programs, like anger management, I have rarely seen as being useful. Assertiveness certainly can be a mannerism, and we all may know too many assertive people. I try to teach that if you understand the situation, and you already know you have all the power in the decision, a smile may be every bit as forceful as a raised voice.

Growth often comes with compliance. The child does not understand the growth potential of a parent/teacher request. My parents insisted

I taste every food item put on my plate, or on the table. They did not insist I eat a large quantity of everything on the table, but they expected me to taste it. When I became rebellious about it, they pushed the issue, and I met with unpleasant consequences. When I was a child I did not understand why they wanted me to taste everything; today, when there are almost no foods I dislike or choose to avoid, but aspic, I understand the reason they wanted this experience for me, and I am deeply appreciative.

"Because I told you to!" Perhaps some of my readers recognize this statement, either because they have said it to their children, or they have heard it from their own parents. It is a well known fact children can push to get the answer they want, and it is not always possible to give them an accurate answer, but I encourage parents to try. Most of the time parents make rules or deny children requests for a reason: *"I do not have the money right now. I am concerned about your safety. In my opinion, you have not earned this request. I am not happy with your badgering me about it, so the answer is no."*

Compliance leads to mastery. Children and most adults do not really understand the nature of compliance; compliance is the mechanism through which one obtains mastery. When I have a particularly non-compliant child in my practice, I will ask if they know the name of the world-wide convention for compilers held every four years. Do you?

It is the Olympics. The Olympics are where compliant people get together to determine who is the best in the world in their area of compliance. Compliance is the mechanism through which people become better at what they do, whether it is related to home work, or the exercises laid out by their coaches. Compliance is what builds performance perfection; it is what makes us superior, and possibly the best.

Apply your heart to discipline, and your ears to words of knowledge. Proverbs 23:12

Children do not understand the reason for practice, or compliance, in their lives. Often parents do not understand key elements related to disciplining, or compliance, either. Parents understand when their children accept discipline—meaning when they accept correction of their behaviors and the punishments associated with their negative behavior—they frequently do not understand compliance expands capability.

Whoever loves discipline loves knowledge Proverbs 12:1

Discipline and compliance allow certain people to become the best in the world. Parents have a tendency to associate compliance with responsibility; compliance is really more of an attribute of accountability than it is of responsibility.

I read somewhere the difference between the average person and the expert in the field is often in the range of 15%. The expert is the person willing to put in 15% more time and energy learning his field than others.

Determination is hard to measure. Even children who have less than the desired level of natural ability can do very well if they are properly motivated. Motivation from inside is the most helpful, but teachers/parents play a major role in this area also.

Grade C thinking: children do not understand how compliance helps them. They feel if they have the general idea it should be enough. I call this *"Grade C thinking."* It is sufficient to get through school, but it does not make for excellence. It does not impress.

I would like to see boys learn to dance and play the piano; girls should learn martial arts and to ride horses. Our children do not understand what is at stake. Parents should consider, along with the child, the areas where compliance is going to be pressed. I do not believe there is a right or wrong to this, but I do believe it is important. Boys need to learn grace. A trait generally not learned on the football field, or the basketball court. Dancing forces them to relate to girls in a more respectful and cooperative manner. A boy who can play a musical instrument will be seen by his female peers as a more valuable, and a more sensitive companion.

Girls and horses go together like syrup on pancakes. Girls seem to need help in the mastery of assertion & timing. My father was a proponent of a person needing to train at least two dogs before even considering raising a child. I think he would have gone along with substituting a horse into the equation. A horse is a big animal to learn to get into sync with. Most women are smaller than their husbands. A horse is one of the dumbest animals on the face of the earth (I think only chickens rank lower). Getting what you want out of a horse requires negotiation. Getting what you want out of a husband requires negotiation. The way to a horse's (man's) heart is through his stomach. A horse (and the average man) does not know the art of finesse around women, and neither will learn if your timing is off. Neither horses, nor men, talk very much, and horses on a whole are probably more affectionate, if you spend time with them.

Timing, conformation, and heart are important aspects of a relationship with a man, or a horse.

Horses and people have natural ways of dealing with happenings. A horse will run if spooked; a child will yell if provoked. A horse can be aggressive about its place in the feeding cycle; when it does not get what it wants, it will become hostile and may start kicking or bucking. A man, if he does not get what he thinks he deserves (food or sex), can also get quarrelsome. Most good trainers could (I am not saying should or do) make a horse look like an outlaw in a few days. An outsider would not know the horse has been trained. Sometimes people, who get horses and do not understand them, find they have a horse performing like an outlaw, and they do not even know what happened, or why. Men can be inadvertently encouraged to be aggressive, also. Women are not responsible for the outcome, but like the horse trainer, they should be aware of ways they might promote an unwanted result.

Training is timing.

The American Psychiatric Association says 50% of Americans will meet the criteria for a mental illness at sometime in their life. Although I do not agree completely with Thomas Stephen Szasz, who wrote <u>The Myth of Mental Illness</u>, I feel labeling 50% of Americans as potentially mentally ill, even if not at the same time, is perhaps an abuse of the process of diagnosis (a psychiatric determination of deviance).

Since approximately 1985-2000, almost everyone gets a diagnosis of Bipolar Disorder if they have seen a psychiatrist, psychologist, or any other person who feels they have the license to make a diagnosis (x-wives). Sixty percent of my practice is children, and if they have been seen professionally, there is a large probability, they will have been diagnosed Bipolar.

Wanting a Bipolar diagnosis is truly a sad state of affairs. Parents have gotten very upset with me when I have not concurred with the diagnosis. Now we have Bipolar I, II, III, IV, V and more recently VI. A psychiatrist in New Mexico suggested the American Psychiatric Association should change its name to the American Bipolar Association. It may happen if proceedings keep going in the direction they are presently headed.

The bottom line is that labeling people (a deviance) puts pressure on both sides of the isle: doctors like giving it; patients frequently demand it. Insurance companies which select which disorders they are willing to pay for unintentionally influence the diagnosis.

Who is selfish, and when are they that way? The word can be used legitimately when it reflects the unwillingness of one party to allow another the same rights and respect the first party demands. I want to ride in the front of the bus, but you cannot have the same right, is selfish. I want to be married to the person I love, but you say I cannot, even though you are married to the person you love, is selfish.

You may not always get what you want; whether we are in the institute of marriage, or government, we need to learn we cannot constantly get our way. Unfortunately, in a Democracy people are often able to align themselves, at least for a while, with the winning side. This is reinforcement for attempting to get our own way. What a nice world it would be if people worked to help others get what they wanted instead of trying to prevent them from getting what they desire. [A book very worthwhile reading on this subject is Actualizations by Stewart Emery.]

Getting what we want is not bad. I do not want the reader to think I believe getting our own way is bad. After all I am an only child. I had a long history of getting my own way.

Developmentally, nature has presented us with a real ongoing challenge. For reasons, one might assume are related to survival of the species, we have been left with a system of thinking commonly present in the first twelve to thirteen years of our lives which is totally inaccurate. The fact we all (all races and genders) have a similar cognitive development makes us relatively blind to the consequences of this erroneous belief system. A lesson for us is the survival of the species may not be as dependent on the accuracy of our belief systems as on the functionality of the belief system.

I would recommend reading the books on cognitive development by Piaget. However, I think he missed something about children's development. He addressed many specific developmental tasks such as when a child can begin to understand concepts such as volume. What he may not have had time to look at was the pervasive belief system running parallel to the findings he illuminated.

This cognitive event is a non-identified **belief** system observed through multiple events of children's lives. The event is the development of an idea or concept—*"Others are responsible for my thoughts, feelings and actions; I am responsible for other's thoughts, feelings, and actions."* Every parent with a child knows the futility of trying to get a child younger than 12-13 years old to *"be responsible"* for events in their lives. Children constantly blame others for whatever happens in their lives. Parents continuously report this problem with their children. Children are actually delusional. Although it may not be politically correct to say so, I have been surprised at how accepting of this declaration my parents have been.

Children accept inconsistencies; almost all child psychiatrists have dealt with children three to seven years of age who have lost a parent, and we expect to find the child believes they were the cause of the parent's death. Children also take on the responsibility for their parent's health, for the divorces in the family, and for nearly all other major or minor events. Children do not have a problem with inconsistencies in their life. They are impressionable, and they do not have an understanding of the world, or how it works. For the first 12.5 years of life, children remain delusional; not as a product of a mental illness, but as a product of development.

NOTE: **This is not said in derogatory terms, nor is it meant to be critical, but it is intended only to help understand the thinking of the child.** They have a belief system of thinking which is inaccurate, and they cannot be talked out of it (before 12.5years). This is the definition of a delusion.

I teach my parents that the **developmental challenge** between the ages of 10 and 12 years is for their children to learn how to ignore those events in life they believe are "making them angry." The exercise of ignoring helps children to begin the process of separating events and feelings. Prior to the age of ten, children weld feelings and events together. The parent says, *"No, you canno go to the movie."* The child feels bad, and they see causality for their hurt feeling in having been told they could not go. In these situations children throw all their energy into getting the parent to change their answer. They believe the parent telling them, *"Yes,"* is the only event able to *"make them"* feel better. They keep banging on the parent in an attempt to get the parent to give them what they feel, and believe, they need. This behavior is reflected in the statement, "If the only tool you have is a jackhammer, you treat the whole world as a slab of concrete."

When children learn not to react to events, they begin to experience that the incident and its accompanying feelings are not one in the same. Events and the following feelings are not casually, but only sequentially, related. This small spacing in time between the event and the feeling allows the person to recognize events have no causal relation to feelings.

When a child can accomplish this task between 10-12.5 years of age, the period from 13-18 is free of most problems. If children do not achieve this developmental task, behaviors and emotions get more problematic every year after the age of twelve: more parent child conflict; more frustration with life; more attacks on the parents (because the parents are the ones perceived as causing the unhappiness); more alienation from the parents; and frequently they begin initiating cutting, or drugs and alcohol use, to take away the perception of pain. The conflicts get worse because the time line of life continues to go on, but the person is stuck in the 10-12 year olds way of unsuccessfully coping: this is the blame way. When stuck in this blame belief system, the child, or adult, just keeps repeating the same error over and over. This error includes the belief that the problem is caused by others, but this perception is almost always incorrect, even when held by the parent or teacher.

One of the paradoxes about this experience is the brighter (higher IQ) the child, the more difficulty they may have in getting out of the blaming system. Bright children have a huge investment in being right. What they do not understand is how the physical and mental worlds run on different principals. Their greater appreciation of the physical world realities does not help them with psychological issues. In fact, it is similar to a carpenter's tools being used for auto repairs. The metaphor is slightly mixed, but would be even more complicated at this point if I did it right. (It is similar to them trying to use carpenter tools to prepare a sermon.) "See I told you so." I will get more into this later.

The problems helping to sustain this error lie in two or three places. One problem is we frequently are not able to see something so pervasive. The second problem is the fact that the error is developmentally grounded, so it is going to be around a long time.

The next problem is educational in nature. Our teachers (home or school) are good at helping children learn how to construct good sentences, but they are not very good about teaching **what sentences do not make any sense**. I warned you I would be bringing up some discussions more than once.

There are at least two reasons for this: the main one being the teachers do not realize what they are failing to do (when options are too prevalent we tend not to see them). The sentence, "The cow jumped over the moon." is a grammatically correct sentence. Outside of the imagination of a nursery rhyme, it does not make any sense. "You make me mad," has a good sentence structure, but it has no more reality than the former sentence. Teachers do not seem to provide this awareness, probably because they do not think about it themselves. Generally, people are very sloppy about what they say and what they tolerate as normal conversation. Example: An event will occur, and the child will say it did not occur. Parents will get into an argument with the child about whether the event occurred, or may see the child as lying. This may continue until someone gets angry, usually the parent; perhaps a better approach would be if the parent would teach the child an improved speaking pattern: If you really do not believe the event happened, I recommend you say something like, "I do not have any memory of that happening, or I do not think it happened." This form of speech is more accurate; it is less inflammatory, and it is much more polite. It is a type of speech likely to keep the speaker out of a lot of trouble throughout their life.

There is a rule: if you say something, you will end up believing it; if you believe something, you will end up acting on it as if it is true. So, when people say, *"You make me mad."* or *"You hurt my feelings."* or *"You made me do it."* they are talking nonsense. These statements are lies when they are referencing psychological issues. You may not like the label, but, at least, be aware it is not accurate speech. These errors of understanding are then turned into errors of behavior. When these errors are criticized, the person manifesting the behavior often has no idea what is wrong, because to them the uncorrected distortion is seen as reality, or as the truth. Most people simply do not understand this.

There is a difference between our physical and our mental worlds. If someone hits you in the arm with a baseball bat, it is legitimate to say, *"He hurt me. He hurt my arm."* This is a physical world cause and effect event. The injury is repeatable. It most likely would cause the same injury if done to 10 people picked randomly. It has science and predictability behind it. It is less subject to mental intermediation. (This factor, mental intermediation, may be present when, or if, a person is embellishing the facts of the physical injury; a condition commonly seen in those seeking disability.)

When it comes to the science of mental injury, there isn't much. I do not expect a lot of my peers to agree with this statement, because we too have been subjected to the pressures by courts and lawyers to buy into the concept. If 10 people experience the same intensity of an event, there will be ten different levels of an outcome, ranging from zero to twelve on a ten-point scale. Lawyers have got to love these cases. They have the opportunity to go for the gold in every case. No one can measure it. No one can replicate it. There is no science related to the findings. No one but *"another expert"* can try to rebut anything said. The real irony is the sicker you are perceived to be, the larger will be your payoff. In this case, it truly pays to be sick, or at least to be perceived to be ill. This is at the heart of why I do not do disability. We tell patients when they call for an appointment, we do not do disability. Occasionally, however, someone will slip through. They are generally recognizable by the fact their symptoms are so exaggerated I am asking myself where is this all coming from, and they tell me they are seeking disability; then I know where is it is coming from.

Is it ever legitimate to consider mental issues as traumatic? **Yes traumas can occur**. There is a condition known as Post Traumatic Stress Disorder (PTSD), and about one in 50 people I see diagnosed with the condition may fit the criteria. This disorder was intended to reflect extreme events, but it has been tamed to where I have seen PTSD claimed because someone said something the person did not like. I have reflected elsewhere on my experience with patients who have claimed psychological injury, and how many seemed to have miraculous recoveries following settlements of their lawsuits.

What is the solution? We need to improve the accuracy of our language, If we speak more accurately, we have less confusion. *"I feel bad,"* is a better statement than *"You make me mad."* Speech is a behavior. Practice of correct speech solves many of the problems people have. A high percentage of the 50% of Americans who will end up with a mental health diagnosis will come from this group, which expressed themselves inaccurately, who believe what they tell themselves, and who will then act on it, as if it is true. They will definitely look deviant. It is not necessary to have another course curriculum for teachers to teach this; it can be taught while teaching everything else.

"To make a man happy do not add to his wealth, but, rather, subtract from his wants." (Stoics) Or, to paraphrase it, as I have heard it, *"Happiness cannot be measured in terms of what we have, but only in terms of freedom from wants."*

Children frequently tell me they are not certain if they are depressed, but they are certain they are unhappy. Over the years, I have had a lot of youngsters who cannot tell the difference between depression and unhappiness. Some cannot tell the difference between depression and tiredness. It is important to be able to distinguish between these conditions, because the treatments are different. Depression can be treated with antidepressants and tiredness with sleep. Unhappiness, on the other hand, must be dealt with by looking at what a person is telling themselves they <u>need</u>. The actual needs we have are air, water, food, shelter and nurturance in children. Other desires labeled needs are strong wants. If they can re-label the intensity, or move, for instance, from need to want, the pain diminishes. The antidote for psychological pain (need) is acceptance. Children have a tendency to be poor acceptors.

We keep pumping off psychological dissidence as long as we stay in need for self, situation, or others to be different from what we believe the situation to be. We frequently refer to this condition as depression, unhappiness, sadness, disappointment, dissatisfaction, displeasure, empty feeling, etc. Note the "believe it to be" which is essential to understand these conditions. Psychological pain is not based on <u>actual</u> events as much as it is on what we <u>believe</u> the reality to be: in other words, mental intermediation.

People are confused by the speed with which they can move from acceptance into need—about the speed of light. They can also move from need back into acceptance at about the speed of sound; sometimes we have to give our mental intermediation a nudge in the correct direction, but we can quickly get there. From the position of acceptance, we are at the door of happiness; we still have to pass through the door to experience it.

Some general recommendations:

SUGGESTIONS ON READING ARTICLES AND BOOKS

There are four concepts one should be aware of when reading, in order to help put knowledge into perspective.

1. What is the level of abstraction being presented in the work? When this characteristic, or attribute, is being considered, it is not a matter of what is right or wrong. There is no right or wrong here. We can accept high or low levels of abstraction; it is only important you understand the level being presented. If one is reading Plato, the information is being presented at a high level of abstraction *("It is the unexamined life that is a waste."* Everything has a *"primary form"* inseparable from the object). These are high-level abstractions, and as such, can have almost an indefinite number of interpretations. The higher the level of abstraction, the harder it is to get agreement. This is why there are over 4,000 Christian denominations in the U.S, and over 24,000 in the world. Everyone thinks his or her interpretation is the correct one. Since there is no way to prove a highly abstract phenomenon, it is not likely there will ever be a consensus. At the other end of abstraction, individuals like Watson, BJ Skinner, Pavlov deal with reactions at the experiential level. Essentially, the premise at this end of the pole of abstraction is the point of view all understanding can be accomplished simply by observing behavior. They believe no real benefit can be accomplished through inserting consciousness onto an event. This is reasoning at a low level of abstraction. There are studies giving credence to the observations. One can study the amount of weight necessary to be added to one hand, before it is perceived as being heavier than the weight in the other hand. Or, how much louder does a sound have to be in order for it to be

perceived as louder than a previous sound. These are measurable and are found to be consistent and repeatable. Is one of these perspectives more accurate than another? No. They are different levels of abstraction through which we examine similar events.

Let me give an example: If you are in a room, look around and see how many places in the room could be considered places to sit. It is likely there would be a high agreement if 10-20 people were asked the same question. Now, let us ask a question of higher abstraction, "Which of the places to sit constitute a *good place to sit?*" Now we may find the level of agreement begins to show cracks. Different people will interpret good in different ways, so the concordance is not going to be as high. Let us move up the pole to a question of, *"What is the best seat in the room?"* At this level of abstraction, we might not have any agreement at all. Each person, for his or her own reasons, might see a different seat as the "best" place to sit. If we understand the level of abstraction, we will have a good idea as to the level of agreement we can expect to get among critics, students, educators, etc.

2. A second thing to consider when reading something is whether the person is using physical world language (change, time, effort, special knowledge, and stability), or psychological world language (no change, no time element, no stability, choice, movement, and selection) language. Is the writer consistent, or does he/she switch back and forth between the languages. The more a person switches back and forth the more confusion there will be in the message presented.

3. The third area of assessment has to do with whether the author is writing from within a childhood system of thinking that others are responsible for my thoughts, feelings, and actions, and I am responsible for other's thoughts, feelings, and actions (I call this System One thinking, because it is the first, or earliest, thought process we structure our life around), or whether the author is writing from the perspective of System Two thinking (a process of thinking becoming available at about 12.5 years of age) which postulates we are each responsible for our own thoughts, feelings

and actions, and others are responsible for their own thoughts, feelings and actions.

If a psychologist wrote a book in which it was asserted people must learn to be vulnerable if they want to be close with others, this writer would be attempting to help people from within system one. Since in System One thinking, person A is seen as responsible for person B's feelings, and person B is seen as responsible for person A's feelings, closeness is seen as generating vulnerability. The solution to the problem is very different if you can identify System One and System Two, and can get out of System One. No one should stay in System One, because if you get out of it and into System Two, closeness is no longer a vulnerable situation. In System Two people can get as close as they want without vulnerability.

Identifying whether a production is being written from the bias of System One, or Two, helps us understand the developmental level of the writer. System One is early childhood thinking, and it generates tremendous problems. System Two, available after twelve and a half, is far more productive, and it actually helps to resolve conflict; System One is a generator of violence and destruction at worse and major unhappiness at best. System One is the basic belief system terrorists ascribe to, and this is one of the reasons I believe terrorists are anti-education. Education can help people learn to think for themselves, bringing at least some into a higher level of problem solving and, thereby, depleting terrorists of their supply of individuals willing to blow themselves up in states of hatred. When you understand you are creating nearly all of your experiences, it is difficult to vehemently hate others because of those experiences. The blame system, in my opinion, is responsible for more deaths than the plague.

4. The fourth perspective to watch out for is the way the writer or individual you are relating to perceives responsibility. Do they use responsibility and accountability interchangeably as a lawyer does, or do they separate responsibility (common usage) into response-ability and assigned accountability? When we use these two concepts, as one concept, it can destroy people's lives (and

commonly does in a court of law) where a careful separation of the concepts can lead to understanding and resolution of conflict.

If we use the concept of response-ability, as the ability to respond, we learn to know anger is a product of our own thinking. If we do not go into blame, we do not create, or experience anger in the first place.

Many outcomes in life are dependent on their beginnings. If we describe events and the cause of events correctly, we will believe them correctly. If we frame our understanding incorrectly, we will believe it incorrectly, and then we will act incorrectly. Say it wrong, think it wrong, and the action on the information will also be wrong.

DEFINITIONS

Learn and use these definitions

Accountability: This is one of the two concepts imbedded in the word responsibility. This word describes the many conventions society has made up to cover situations. It may apply to others (Assigned Accountability) or to our self (Self-accountability). Internal and external factors may have little or no influence on when it is used.

Assigned Accountability: Accountability may be assigned either to self (Self-accountability) or to others or even to events. Others may assign accountability to you or to themselves: often incorrectly. Accountability is a convention (It is essentially made up). Attributes of Assigned Accountability are:

> **It is frequently fixed.**
> **It is not influenced directly by internal or external factors.**

There are three actions we are commonly held responsible (meaning accountable) for or we hold ourselves responsible (meaning accountable) for:

> **Other people's thoughts**
> **Other people's feelings**
> **Other people's behaviors**

Blame System (S1T): The Blame System is the way children are hard wired to see the world for the first 12.5 years of their lives. The Cardinal belief of childhood is "Others are response-able for (create) my thoughts, feelings and actions; I am "response-able" for (create) others thoughts, feelings and actions." I sometimes refer to this as the early *"operating system"* of childhood.

Cause and Effect: Generally a physical relationship where A causes B to happen. This concept is often mistakenly applied to psychological events. The concept frequently confused with it is sequential ordering of events.

Change thinking: When I use these words I am reflecting on the form of thinking requiring a new choice for them to get better. It grounds one in the physical world thinking, preventing one from using much more powerful psychological words like choice, movement or selection.

Choice: This is a psychologically powerful word helping to ground a person in psychological thinking. This is the concept you want to hold in your mind when you desire to get results. Its companion words are movement and selection.

Control: Control is a concept almost always present simultaneously with change. If I can truly change, or make an outcome different from what nature intends, it may be useful to apply the word control. In most situations there is neither control, nor change, and the use of these words again grounds one in the Physical World Paradigm.

Depression: This is a word having both psychological and physical meanings. It can refer to a flat affect, unhappy mood state, or to the physiological depressant action drugs, like alcohol, may have on the neurological system.

Guilt: Guilt is the body feeling created when we are unwilling to pay the price related to the decisions we make. It has no actual relationship to the rightness or wrongness of a thought or an action. It is sometimes used by the unscrupulous or unknowing to manipulate others, especially children.

Inaccurate speech: Speech not conveying accurately the reality of a situation.

Mental Intermediation: This is the thinking/processing going on in the mind between an event and a reaction to the event. It is largely ignored. It is generally left out of the description of the cause of events and feelings. It is the source of most of the feelings people experience in life. It is not recognized by the blamers. It is recognized by people who show a higher degree of self-accountability.

Operating System: I am usurping this word from computer language to mean essentially the same function at a human level. The operating system in a computer is what tells it how to behave. The operating systems in humans also direct our thoughts and actions.

Other accountability (Blame): When we attribute an issue or cause of an issue to other or others.

Physical World: This is a reference to the material world. This is the world of items composed of atoms.

Physical World Paradigm: This is a reflection of the way most people see change occurring in the physical world: Time is required. Energy is required. Special knowledge is often required. The product is considered stable. Applied to psychological events it is a time consuming disaster.

Problem Solving System: This is another way of describing System 2 Thinking (S2T)

Psychological World: This is the world of ideas, thoughts, and intangibles. It is not the world of the physical. This world is largely the product of the mechanism of the brain referred to as thinking. In this world options are neither created nor destroyed.

Psychological World Paradigm: This refers to the way people can understand the psychological world in contrast to the physical world. In the psychological world a time element does not apply. The energy expenditure is either neutral or non-existent. There is no need for special knowledge only a need to recognize we already have the knowledge needed. There is no stability beyond what can be established by habit.

Responsibility: As generally used this word implies choice and compliance at the same time. It suggests mobile and fixed event at the same time. It encourages the assignment of blame and discourages understanding. It is the form of the word loved by many attorneys. In this book it means the undifferentiated form of the word.

Response-ability: This is one of the two concepts imbedded in the word Responsibility. It has to do with awareness plus capability. It is what we have 100% of the ability to do, without other's help. Response-ability is capability + awareness. Its attributes are:

> **It is constantly in flux.**
> **It cannot be transferred.**
> **Internal issues such as strength & IQ influence it.**
> **It is influenced by external factors such as tools.**
> **There are three actions we are response able for:**
> **Our own thoughts**
> **Our own feelings**
> **Our own behaviors**

Self-accountability: This is one form of assigned accountability [which is one of the two concepts imbedded in the word responsibility.] It has to do with what we have 100% of the ability to do without other's help (response-ability), plus what we can possibly influence to happen. [response-ability+Influence] Visualize two circles, one inside the other. The center circle is response-ability and the circle around it is the sphere of influence.

Self-accountability System/Problem Solving System: This is the way of thinking available after the age of 12 years. Its premise is *"I am response-able for my thoughts, feelings, and actions; others are response-able for their own thoughts, feelings, and actions."* This SHOULD be the operating system of adults.

Sequential Ordering of Events: When events happen one after the other in time or in form but are not caused by what went first: i.e. B follows A in the alphabet but is not caused by A. Commonly confused with cause and effect.

<u>Shame</u>: Shame is the body feeling experienced when our assessment of self and our image of self do not match.

<u>System One Thinking</u> (S1T): I call this system one thinking because it appears to me to be the first organizing belief system children develop. I also refer to this as an <u>operating system</u> because of the way it helps determine outcomes (products generated by our thoughts can be action and/or feelings). The root of System 1 Thinking is "Others are responsible for (create) my thoughts, feelings and actions; I am responsible for (create) others thoughts, feelings and actions.

<u>System Two Thinking</u> (S2T): I call this "system two thinking" because it is the second organizing belief system becoming available at about 12.5 years of age. I also refer to this as an <u>operating system</u> because of the way it helps determine the products generated. The root of S2T is "I am responsible for (create) my thoughts, feelings and actions; others are responsible for (create) their thoughts, feelings and actions. This system of thinking does not occur as a linear part of development in System 1 Thinking and people can go through their entire life and not be aware of S2T. It is a competitive processing system-think of Beta vs. VHS, or Mac vs. PC—becoming available at around 12 years of age. Unlike the case for Mackintosh or PC computers, there is no announcement by nature when it is available, and no one, including our educational system, makes its appearance a publicized event. System 2 thinking must be accessed in order to be useful.

It is best to correct distortions by identifying them; not by identifying them as transference reactions, but through the process of identifying the thinking process causing a problem. When a student/patient challenges me over who is right, my response is I have no idea who is right, but I do have a lot of experience hearing what people have to say about what I have suggested they do, and on the whole, they report it makes their life much more enjoyable. I encourage them to be aware they have a choice about their response to me. Like the horse brought to water, they can either drink, or make a mess. I attempt to make it clear right off it is not my business which way they choose to go, I am only concerned they know they have a choice, and what some of those outcomes will likely be to the different choices.

Please contact me at rapidreliefseries.com if you interested
in setting up a conference on any of the topics discussed.

BOOKS BY THE AUTHOR

Rapid Relief from Emotional Distress Revised

Rapid Relief Series: Book 1 a book for people who suffer.

Excerpt

I have undertaken to rewrite aspects of the original book because, with time, comes further insights. I also wanted to reduce the size of the book, so not only the information but the book itself would reflect a more rapid event. When I see a book advocating rapid relief and it is over 250 pages long, I think it will take me too long just to read it. I have also made a small change in the manner of reporting. It appears socially correct for counselors, therapists, and psychologists to refer to people they work with as clients. The designation seems too commercial, or impersonal, and does not sit well with me, and because of that, when I am referring to individuals I work with they are referred to by the time-tested designation of patient. The reference to people as patients does not in any way intend to demean anyone, or exalt anyone, but is a reflection of the very special bond that doctor and patient have enjoyed since the birth of medicine, and which managed care is doing its best to destroy.

When I entered the real world, I was not prepared by my training to treat the many patients who needed medicine. Then, I found a form of therapy reducing my need to use medications by nearly half, or more. Currently, I see people being severely over treated for conditions described as metabolic, or medical, which I routinely treat using brief psychotherapy interventions. In the thirty-nine years I have been in practice I have seen the pendulum swing from one extreme to another; I like neither.

I have elected to alter the format of this book, from the original, in a couple ways; I hope I have created a more readable edition. I have separated out the basic information I want everyone to know, from both the Exercises and Case Reports. It is my hope the information will be more quickly accessible to the reader. Dr. Emery and I originally conceived a book having about 150 pages. The original editors, however, had other ideas, and they won. This was why a lot of the exercises and case reports were added. Since it was published, people have commented to me about the book, and I was somewhat surprised at how often they commented positively about the exercises. I did not want to exclude them in this version, but I did want the exercises to stand on their own merit. Therefore, I created an internet site (rapidreliefseries@cox.com) where those who are interested can get a copy of the workbook for a small fee.

Psychological Therapy in a Pharmacological World

Book 2 in the Rapid Relief Series-a book for doctors, therapists, and anyone in therapy wanting to speed up the process.

Excerpt

It has been said that doctors go to scientific meetings to learn what their colleagues can teach them, and they go to the office to learn what their patients can teach them. Simply put, this book is a reflection on some of the lessons I have learned from my patients and other people in my life. What I have learned in brief is that much of what I was taught in my psychiatric residency and child fellowship is not very useful. I have not come to bury psychiatry, but I hope to wake it up.

I chose to become a doctor that would work with the mind when I was five years of age. I did not learn that one of the names for people who did that was psychiatrist until many years later. In the small town of

Warsaw, Illinois, population of 2000 there were no psychiatrist, or for that matter, there were no psychologists either. How the mind worked was a curiosity to me then, and it still intrigues me today.

I have observed that professional training often brings about a narrowing of one's perspective, rather than broadening it. I have experienced this when I talk with other colleagues (doctors) about my experience and the points of view I have about treating patients. I get a far narrower response from psychiatrists, therapists, counselors than when I discuss these ideas with non-professionals. While I was at UCLA for my child fellowship, I tried to present several of these concepts to staff members there. With the blessed exception of Gary Emery Ph.D., I found no one was very interested in my observations. I get letters and calls from patients and non-patients who tell me how Dr. Emery and my book Rapid Relief from Emotional Distress opened up an entirely new approach to living for them. Yet, even in a time when therapy is not being paid for by many insurance companies, when there is a shortage of trained professionals, and I have a type of therapy that not only works, but is compatible with the typical short appointment times, I have not been able to mobilize much interest in the medical community.

Theology Simplified: Why do we make understanding so complicated?

Book 4 in the Rapid Relief Series-a book for thinkers

Excerpt

The Neanderthal may have had some thoughts about the afterlife. Some seemed to bury their dead, and they left items in the graves, presumably because they thought they might be needed in the next life. With a better mind came more thoughts being directed to looking for understanding. The advance in brain power must have been like getting a new toy to play with.

At that point, Homo sapiens may have turned in a direction not in their best interest. They traded in the experiential life for the contemplative life. Why do I label it as possibly unfortunate? Because we got so enamored with the pursuit of knowledge about God before we had any real rules of science to follow. By the time people were actually thinking about how they were thinking, theology had already staked out a claim on part of the world of thought, and the church was able to frighten enough of the world through secrecy and intimidation (actually bullying and torture) to prevent a major challenge of the system, except from within (Luther). After all when you can either burn someone at the stake who does not believe the same way you do, or you can threaten to prevent them from ever getting into heaven, you are bound to sway some folks.

Perhaps you will be among those who believe the challenge should still come from within. I am not a theologian, so I am not on the inside. I have spent a great deal of my professional life attempting to look at speech and speech patterns, and at the way speech generates beliefs which then becomes the bases for the behavior. As a psychiatrist looking at the arguments of theology which have been with us for thousands of years, there is only one phrase that comes to mind: mental gibberish.

ACKNOWLEDGMENTS

I wish to thank the following people:

My wife Sharon Campbell who has tolerated my hours of writing, and rewriting, and for her help in the final editing of all my books.

KC Koestner for his work in creating the cover for this book and the other Rapid Relief Series books, and Suzanne (Shelly) Koestner for helping with the formatting tasks and getting the completed manuscript to the publisher.

CONTACTS

James E. Campbell, M.D.
Distinguished Life Fellow
American Psychiatric Association
American Board of Psychiatry and Neurology
14015 N. 51st Avenue
602-439-2400
Rapidreliefseries.com
Glendale, Arizona 85306

Gary Emery, Ph.D.
Los Angeles Center for Cognitive Therapy
630 s. Wilton Place
Los Angeles, California 90005
213-387-4737

The internet site (rapidreliefseries@cox.com) contains information on books and materials that are available. I am also available for conferences on any of the subject matter. It is my intent to eventually have audio presentations for each book.

CPSIA information can be obtained
at www.ICGtesting.com
Printed in the USA
LVHW090538161020
668980LV00001B/28